New Dimensions in Philosophical Theology

Edited by
Carl A. Raschke

Journal of the American Academy of Religion Studies

Volume XLIX, Number 1

GENERAL EDITOR: Robert P. Scharlemann, University of Virginia
ASSISTANT TO THE EDITORS: Mary Lou Doyle

☐ The Cover _____

The intersecting lines in the graphic sign represent the action of religious reality (the vertical line) upon the world of ideas (the horizontal line) by going back to the origin (the dot) from which reality and ideas come. In a general way, this is the intention of the Journal's thematic series in religious studies.

Manufactured in the United States of America

Contents

Editor's Preface   v

I.   The "Religious" Subject Matter in Philosophical Reflection   1

   1. Toward a Science of Religion   *David R. Crownfield*   3

   2. Three Types of Reasoning in Religion   *Peter Slater*   17

II.   The Perplexities of Theological Endeavor   35

   3. Argument in Theology: Analogy
      and Narrative   *David B. Burrell*   37

   4. Morality, Judgment, and Prayer   *Robert O. Johann*   53

III.   Theology and the Moment of Deconstruction   71

   5. Metaphor and the Accession to
      Theological Language   *Charles E. Winquist*   73

   6. G N I C A R T
      T R A C I N G   *Mark C. Taylor*   85

   7. The Image of the Beast, or Theology
      and the Thought of Difference   *Carl A. Raschke*   109

Notes on Contributors   127

THE CONTRIBUTORS

DAVID B. BURRELL
Department of Theology
University of Notre Dame
Notre Dame, IN 46556

DAVID R. CROWNFIELD
Department of Philosophy & Religion
University of Northern Iowa
Cedar Falls, IA 50613

ROBERT O. JOHANN
Department of Philosophy
Fordham University
Bronx, NY 10458

CARL A. RASCHKE
Department of Religious Studies
University of Denver
Denver, CO 80208

PETER SLATER
Department of Religion
Carleton University
Ottawa, Ontario, Canada

MARK C. TAYLOR
Department of Religion
Williams College
Williamstown, MA 01267

CHARLES E. WINQUIST
Department of Religious Studies
California State University
Chico, CA 95927

The following volume of essays was originally chartered as a series of *Gedankenversuche* within a region of inquiry which over the past few decades has become somewhat blurred and diffuse. The locution "philosophical theology" has become noticeably ambiguous in both connotation and force, not only because its constituent terms have lost much of their previously precise meaning, but also by virtue of the growing confusion surrounding what counts as a theological issue which might be leavened or qualified by the insights of philosophy *per se*. In an era when the inscriptions on the old methodological boundary stones have weathered away, any attempt simply to rework traditional problems and materials must prove to be a futile venture, even if the measure of critical self-consciousness has been raised to a maximal height and the intentions remain unabashedly sincere. As William Butler Yeats has put it, "things thought too long can no longer be thought." The adage holds for the theological disciplines as well, including that variable domain of thinking known as "philosophy of religion" or "philosophical theology." In such a setting the proper agenda of thinkers tutored in the traditional tasks is to redraw the maps of the terrain. Hence, the title of this anthology denotes not new "approaches" so much as new "dimensions."

The first group of essays deals with the broad, taxonomical question of religion in itself in so far as it arises as a subject matter for philosophical examination, as opposed to historical and descriptive accounts. David Crownfield takes up the issue of the religious "experience" as it discloses itself in the intersection between traditional phenomenology and transpersonal psychology. Peter Slater's article concerns the way in which religious or theological "reasoning" gives direction and contour to an implicit pattern of symbols, i.e., a *mythos*.

The second section touches on specific philosophical dilemmas begotten from theological investigation. David Burrell's piece explores the linkage between what is conventionally regarded as theological "argumentation" and the narrative framework of religious tradition. Robert Johann looks at the classical problem of God's existence in the altogether "pragmatic" light of everyday religious conduct and devotion.

The third segment introduces some deliberately unsystematic reflections on what might be termed theology's own contemporary "deconstruction." Deconstruction (the term was first given currency by Jacques Derrida) is a movement in thought which betokens the "end" of a particular tradition. Charles Winquist ponders the movement of deconstruction with particular attention to theological writing and the hermeneutics of metaphor. Mark Taylor undertakes an exercise in deconstruction itself. And, last of all, Carl Raschke aims us toward the "apocalyptic" finale anticipated in the initial moment of deconstructive energy.

These essays, therefore, are thematically woven together by a common response to the sense of "crisis" or of the need for new discernments, rather than by consistency of topic areas. The reader must take these articles not as gratuitous nuggets to be exchanged for edification or some spurious "enlightenment," but as bridgeheads perhaps toward a different shore.

I.
The "Religious" Subject Matter in Philosophical Reflection

Toward a Science of Religion

David R. Crownfield

It has been eighty years since William James presented his Gifford Lectures on *The Varieties of Religious Experience*. His respect for the integrity and diversity of the materials and his open-minded treatment of the reality-status of what is experienced have scarcely been equalled in the meantime. Indeed, many treatments of the subject have opted either, in the tradition of Feuerbach, to reduce religious experience to a naturalistic base fully understood from nonreligious contexts, or, as in the primordialism of Huston Smith, to reduce them to a single, normative theological model. James, to the contrary, insisted on a patient and descriptive attention to the differentia as well as to the commonalities of the experiences (25f.). In its empiricist deference to the data, its renunciation of dogmatic predefinitions, its overall open-mindedness, James's method was appropriately scientific. He differentiates his treatment from that of "the sciences of nature" on the ground that their materialism entails a bias against the claims of religion, and thus constitutes another dogmatic foreclosure of the empirical task (490).

In proposing to resume the characterization of the study of religion as a science, I do so in James's spirit. I do not intend a technical argument about what does and does not constitute a true science—an exercise of more interest to metatheorists than to those actually engaged in scientific inquiry. I propose to indicate some of the procedures of descriptive inquiry into the nature and diversity of religious experience. I propose to identify some of the domains of relevant data that have become available in recent years. And I propose to identify a set of critical difficulties in the way of achieving an open and objective view of the phenomena.

The method of a science of religion must be phenomenological. That is, it must bring to light the ordering characteristics of the phenomena as they disclose themselves, rather than treat them as causal derivatives of some predefined set of "real" elements. "Subjective" and "objective," "immanent" and "transcendent," function in such a phenomenology as experiential characteristics *within* the phenomena, rather than as explanatory devices extrinsic to them (Otto). "The Otherness of God," in this approach, is a characteristic of some religious experiences and not of others, and need not be treated as a metaphysical proposition whose truth or falsity is to be proven from the data.

A science of religion must be not only a phenomenological but a hermeneutic science. The texts which narrate religious experiences pose profound and central problems of interpretation. Questions of meaning, the functions of symbol and of ambiguity, the role of tradition in constituting a horizon of interpretation, cannot be left out of account. The hermeneutic circle in which every interpretation is a self-interpretation is nowhere more central than here where the nature and value of self is itself at stake (Crownfield, 1979). The phenomenological and the hermeneutic character of the science of religion are interdependent, each clarifying and focussing the other (Ihde). Clearly such a method will never attain the mathematical formality characteristic of a number of "strict" sciences. It can, however, be disciplined by unprejudiced openness, by a norm of consensus, and by the corrective authority of the data.

To approach the study of religion by a phenomenological-hermeneutic method permits us to avoid a number of problems that have, in the past, tended to obstruct the enterprise. It is characteristic of a wide variety of religious experiences that they assert the givenness of an object, a noema, a spiritual reality. To premise the study of religion on the denial of such objects or realities (Larson) imposes on the phenomena a dogmatic preconception, as James recognized. To assume, on the other hand, that some theology or metaphysics provides a normative paradigm for experiences that are, on their face, diverse (Smith) does the same thing from the other side. In both cases, the question of truth is predetermined in examining the evidence. A phenomenological approach permits both the likenesses and the unlikenesses, both the elsewhere-known and the religion-specific, to show themselves.

The problem of the object in religious experience is not abolished by a phenomenological-hermeneutic approach. But it is the intrinsic problem, of the object-which-shows-itself, rather than the extrinsic issue of the object "behind" the phenomena. But the religious object-which-shows-itself is, by all accounts, problematic and elusive. God discloses himself contingently, to whom and as he will (Barth). Especially at the hands of those scholars of religion for whom, as for James (539), "I have no such commerce [with a higher consciousness or God]—I wish I had, but I can't close my eyes to its vitality in others," it is not obvious how the phenomenon is to be made accessible to the phenomenology. If I do not have access to the object of study for my discipline, it is questionable whether I am qualified to pursue it.

Some years ago, at a meeting of the American Academy of Religion, and in reaction to a particular constellation of papers, I found myself troubled by a strange sensation. It was as though we were all beginning to suspect that our field was about something after all, and it was something we knew nothing about. This was, in a sense, a fantasy of the moment, but it has an element of truth. If, indeed, religious documents and behavior are based on experiences of a sort to which many people have access, and if we are not among them, we are in a very anomalous position as professionals.

There are two directions that we can follow in hope of moving out of this predicament. On the one hand, we can undertake a careful hermeneutical analysis of the texts, and of the problems of understanding the texts, which should at least make explicit the distance between our standpoint and that of the texts and examine the limits of the possibility of our opening ourselves to a disclosure from the texts (Crownfield, 1979). On the other hand, we can submit ourselves to the requisite techniques and/or disciplines in pursuit of the direct experiences themselves. This approach is not without its own very serious problems, however. One such problem, as the paper in the preceding reference develops, is that classic texts of religious experience include explicit statements that the understanding of those experiences is problematic precisely for the person undergoing the experience. It is an irony not to be avoided that the experiences we now do not understand because we *do not* experience them would become even more centrally problematic for the understanding if we *did* experience them. This does not, I believe, make the direct experience either fruitless or irrelevant to our inquiry. It is true that such an outcome calls into question the whole nature of human understanding and the notion of the primacy of direct experience. But it is just this sort of challenge which the classic accounts of religious experience attribute to the self-manifestation of the religious object. It may be that the project of achieving an access to the object which does not disrupt the standpoint of the investigator is impossible as a necessary consequence of the nature of this sort of object. If so, then it is precisely the insistence that the object of our study be given to the discipline in a way of which we are masters that precludes our access to it. By insisting that we understand as autonomous authorities the object of our study, we make it impossible to understand.

Clearly the predicament in which this reflection has landed us makes the project of a "science" of the religious object severely problematical. To extend the problem a bit, let us take account of the fact that all the classic testimonies concerning the self-manifestation of the religious object are in agreement that the object, the god, discloses itself in contingent and particular contexts, by a specific name, for the most part through specified procedures to a specific community (or more rarely to arbitrarily-determined individuals who then initiate a new community). As we seek to move out of the dilemmas of an empty and universal autonomy with respect to our discipline we move into a contrary set of problems of particularity. If the object of our study is only accessible in contingent and particular contexts, then how is a universal science of that object possible at all?

This problem is a special and central form of a general difficulty intrinsic to any project of understanding. Every project of understanding begins in preconception, in misunderstanding and absence of understanding, without which there would be neither a need for a project of understanding, nor a beginning place from which to go forward (Gadamer:235f.). Every project, then, of understanding the object of religious experience begins in the particularities, the preconceptions, and the ignorances of a contingent starting-point. That contingency and absence are affirmed by the texts to be intrinsic to the self-manifestation of this object (Barth:184f.) serves as a warning against premature abstraction and generalization. It may, indeed, be a permanent difficulty and limit to the project of a science of religion.

There is, however, no absolute barrier to understanding in the contingent diversity of interpreter and text. Full closure of the difference is absolutely impossible, but articulation of that coming-together in which the limit is encountered, and of the configuration of the impasse itself, is a proper and central sort of act of interpretation. In the hermeneutical fusion of horizons between the interpreter and the interpreted, it is not impossible, even—indeed, especially—at the point of impasse, to recognize the equal cohumanity of the other, and the equal validity of the other's mode of experience. This recognition, too, will be imperfect and partial. Methodology has no solutions for human finitude and fallibility. It may be that we got into this business out of the lust to be gods, but it is clear that that lust interferes with the attainable objective of achieving some degree of understanding of the nature and object of religious experience.

In addition to the *aporiae* intrinsic to understanding the religious object, there remains to be noted the fact that access to the religious object through the interpretation of accounts of another's experience does not entail the adoption of the other's theology or metaphysics. We might conclude, indeed, that the experience is object-related, but that the object was quite different than the witness supposed. For Jung, for example, images of God are images of the self. To understand encounters with God is not to deal with supernatural beings, whatever the subject may believe, but to encounter the self. Self, for Jung, is of course, not the empirical "me" or ego, but the archetypal concept of totality, of the ideal unification of all the elements of the psyche. With respect to the actually attained unification, this archetype stands as phenomenologically other, transcendent, numinous, exercising a revelatory and transformative power over the ego from "beyond." It is experienced as God precisely because it is the self. In addition to being an example of understanding the object while amending the description, Jung's position also illustrates the concept of a science of religion in another respect. If his thesis is true, it entails that inquiry into the experience of the transcendent and phenomenological inquiry into the structures of the psyche, conducted independently, should prove to be convergent. This is, in a broad sense, an empirical as well as a hermeneutical inquiry, and is thus an instance for the thesis that the question of the nature of the object of religious experience is susceptible to empirical examination.

Neither a self-legitimizing insider-account nor a reductive outsider-account of religion can meet the basic requirement of a science in the broadest sense: an inquiry governed by its object in a manner equally accessible to all competent, open, and disinterested inquirers. If such a requirement is to be met, it must be met in a way which preserves the insider's respect for the contingent self-disclosure of the object as well as the outsider's demand that the object be intelligible within the domain of intelligible objects at large. It must preserve the disinterested nature of scientific inquiry generally: that there are no privileged or preselected outcomes of the investigation. Yet as a phenomenological and hermeneutical science it also must conform to the requirement that any interpretive enterprise must be premised on the recognizable possibility of the disclosure of the object within the interpreter's own experiential horizon. This conformity must, in one way or another, take account of the claim in the texts that the object discloses itself only within the particular religious community, and at the same time must not confine the possibility of understanding to participants in that community.

The claim that the object of religious experience can be subjected to disciplined investigation requires that we explicate more fully where there is to be found evidence bearing on the question, by what procedures the evidence is to be rendered accessible to our reflection, and what are to be the canons of interpretation to be engaged with the evidence. I propose, in brief, that the evidence consists of first-hand experience, direct testimony, and the texts of the traditions; that the methods of access be experiment, participant observation, interview, and exegesis, specifically including psychohistorical and critical modes of interpretation, and that the interpretive engagement be essentially that of an existential hermeneutics of being there.

It is a dozen years since Walter Pahnke's briefly famous article, "Drugs and Experimental Mysticism," proposed that religious experiences be experimentally explored through the use of psychedelic chemicals. The problem with Pahnke's proposal was that there appeared to be no ground for regarding the analogies between mystical experience and psychedelic experience positively. Either they were accidental toxic products and of no significance for understanding "true" religious experience, or they seem to imply that mysticism itself was merely such a toxic accident, perhaps induced in traditional instances by other chemical or physiological agents than hallucinogenic drugs, but in any case of no real significance except to psychopharmacologists. (As Walter was doing his dissertation on psilocybin and mystical experience, I was doing mine on the doctrine of man, as we then called it, in Karl Barth's theology. I was confident that the most significant implication that could possibly come from Pahnke's work would be a confirmation of Barth's general rejection of religion as a human project inherently incapable of bringing people into relation to God.)

Since the publication of Stanislav Grof's research with LSD (1975, 1977, 1980) the situation has been profoundly changed. Grof's findings indicate, and on this point independent research from several other points of view confirms, that the experiential content of psychedelic experience is not drug-specific, but rather dependent on the basic structure and personality of the subject. Grof also indicates, as do other writers, that all the specific contents of the psychedelic experience occur also in sensory-isolation experiences, in non-drug-related trance conditions such as those developed by Houston and Masters, and in deep hypnosis, as well as in meditative and mystical experiences, in mythology, and in a variety of ritual contexts. Grof concludes, and I agree, that psychedelics simply provide a technology for rendering accessible in an intense way experiences of sorts that are otherwise known but more difficult to produce at will. The drug, he holds, functions as a nonspecific amplifier of deep psychic processes. These processes not only are found in non-drug contexts; psychedelic research indicates that they are much more central and fundamental to our common human reality than the relative rarity of such special experiences would suggest. It is that centrality combined with the high incidence of religious imagery and affect in these experiences and the close analogies with the structures of more-traditional religious experiences, that signals the great importance for us of Grof's findings (Crownfield, 1976).

There are, of course, serious difficulties in the way of religious research with LSD. The legal obstacles are not, indeed, the most important. The psychological impact of bringing into consciousness structures and affects which are deeply repressed and which underlie the foundations of the ego which must try to cope with them can be extremely dangerous. Such a research program, if legal obstacles were to be overcome, could only safely be carried out with careful psychiatric oversight and in a context in which the priority of human values and mutual commitment took clear precedence over experimentalism and manipulative distancing. In the meantime, of course, there remains the exegetical and hermeneutical enterprise of interpreting Grof's published results.

Those who, like Zaehner, believe that to include drug-induced experiences in the domain of study of religion and to compare them to classic mystical experiences "is in fact denying any specific religious basis to either Hinduism or Christianity" (83), need neither be permitted to veto this whole line of inquiry nor be dismissed out of hand. Zaehner, indeed, subjects the text of Huxley's experience to critical examination, and engages in a personal exploration of the domain in dispute. His results, like Huxley's and Grof's are part of the domain of evidence to be studied. If there are observable differences between psychedelic and classically mystical experiences, they need to be explicated. If there are observable similarities, they must not be ignored. Openness, not a rush to judgment, is the hallmark of good science. The questions are empirical, and the answers must fall where they may.

Following the lead of Grof's assertion that all the major results of psychedelic research can also, though sometimes less clearly or efficiently, be attained by other means, it is appropriate to consider some other specific methods by which the proposed inquiry might go forward.

With Grof's mapping of his own results as a reference point, it should be possible to make significant advances through the use of such non-drug methods. Jean Houston and Robert Masters, after making major contributions to the early stages of psychedelic research in this country, have for the last fifteen years continued their work using non-drug methods. Research using their various procedures, including the lotos cradle (a 360-degree pendulum suspended, like Socrates in "The Clouds," between heaven and earth), should make a significant contribution to the problem. Alice Pempel, in her unpublished Fordham dissertation, has provided an analysis and mapping of some of Houston and Master's material which gives as clearly ordered an account of some of the outer reaches of human experience as I have seen. Pempel's analysis of this material, however, has led her to express in personal communications the judgment that the Houston-Masters techniques are also not without psychological and spiritual risks. She proposes that the necessary safeguards against such risks are essentially those included in the traditional spiritual disciplines. Any attempt to mature a science of religion would clearly have to examine those disciplines in the course of formalizing the appropriate safeguards. Such an approach would require that a clear distinction be made between the spiritual duties of a science of religion and the ordinary ethical responsibilities of experimental psychology. The participants in a laboratory study of religious experience would have to be committed seekers, and the existential and spiritual centrality for their lives of the study being carried out would have to be kept clearly in mind throughout, and respected, if not shared, by the investigators themselves. A corollary of this would be the principle so clearly articulated and faithfully followed in John Lilly's researches: no research methods are to be used in which the researcher herself or himself has not fully participated. This principle has not only ethical but hermeneutical import. To understand another's report of experience is to understand in it a possibility for my own existence. We cannot study spiritual experiences and states about which those who have experienced them report that they find themselves ultimately at risk in the experience without being prepared to accept that risk ourselves, lest we adopt interpretations of their experience which function precisely to protect us against having to take the risk, and thus to prevent us from understanding.

John Lilly is himself another investigator whose work must be taken seriously in this inquiry. Lilly's own interpretations are idiosyncratic and his methods eclectic, but he does provide a number of significant pieces for our puzzle. Adequate phenomenological and hermeneutical clarification of his accounts of his explorations can serve to extract further insights. Lilly's most important methodological contribution is the invention of a reasonably compact and inexpensive sensory isolation chamber, and the demonstration that such a chamber provides access to some of the important sorts of experience we need to study. In effect, the isolation chamber eliminates from the study of meditation and related issues the problems of the stable posture and the straight spine, and the associated gravity stresses on the body, and permits relatively prompt and easy access to meditative states of consciousness./1/

Important though direct laboratory study of religion is for our questions, it would be provincial and short-sighted for researchers in religion to confine themselves to evidence we can generate ourselves. There exist in the contemporary world a wide variety of both traditional and experimental communities practicing disciplines aimed at the generation of religious or quasi-religious experiences. The Tibetan centers, Naropa at Boulder and Nyingma at Berkeley, the Zen monasteries at Shasta and Tassajara, Muktananda's ashrams, Jack Kornfeld's Theravada center in Massachusetts, as well as the Christian contemplative orders, come immediately to mind both as sources for subjects for interview and as centers for participant observership.

There has been considerable controversy in recent years concerning Trungpa's method and personal style at Naropa Institute, especially centering on his encounter with W. S. Merwin on Hallowe'en, 1975 (Sanders). These matters, in context of the life of the community in which they occur, and with an interpretive perspective informed by Trungpa's own work and the Tantric tradition, are a proper subject of study. Not only psychedelic and lotos-cradle approaches to spiritual experiences are dangerous. Danger is inherent in the enterprise, and Pempel's cautions apply to all its forms. Whether, in this instance, the prey of the dangers is Merwin, or Trungpa, or both, may be necessarily ambiguous to the outsider. But the problems are proper and intrinsic to our discipline and need to be addressed.

Among contemporary nontraditional movements, I will mention two examples. Oscar Ichazo's Arica training combines Sufi elements with components of the Gurdjieff program. John and Eva Peirrakos seek to integrate bioenergetic therapy, now modified to a sort of western Hatha Yoga, with spiritualistic and meditative practices. There is a wealth of material at hand to study; what is lacking seems to be a combination of the will and the method, to both of which I hope this paper speaks.

The whole strange in-between area calling itself "transpersonal psychology" needs in this connection to be given closer scrutiny than most scholars of religion have yet been willing to give. The transpersonal psychologists are, in large part, uncritical literalists about reports of out-of-body experiences, or dying-and-returning, or remembering past lives, or visiting other realms of being. They tend to be panpsychists or some other sort of idealists, and a great many are immortalists, raising a question about the extent to which they have or have not come to terms with their own death and their embodiment. Once again, as with Lilly, what we need to do is to subject their reports to systematic phenomenological and hermeneutical clarification. A theologian looks to them not for theoretical models but for experiential materials. Something is apparently happening in our own world which is curiously similar in a number of respects to what our familiar old texts tell about, and we are paying it little or no attention. Kenneth Ring has done a disciplined study of the issues raised in Moody's *Life After Life*. Work presumably goes on in the territory popularized in Monroe's *Journeys Out of the Body*, and with respect to "reincarnational memories." It is clear that those who report, and especially those who popularize, these matters tend to claim a kind of metaphysical literalism which is embarrassing to a critical philosopher of religion. But that same sort of literalism characterizes our primary textual materials from the past. Why should we insist on studying experiential reports only from dead people from other cultures? Sometimes it seems that it is precisely the guaranteed otherness of the traditional materials that secures our own immunity from existential risk in our study—an immunity which is at the same time an assurance that we do not understand what we are interpreting.

So far, I have proposed four domains of evidence for a possible science of religion. We must study carefully the new technological resources available for providing experimental access to ranges of experience related to our traditional domain. We must combine such experimental studies with a discipline of personal self-exploration, placing ourselves at risk and acquiring the necessary first-hand knowledge of the basic phenomena under study. We must examine the practices and experiences of contemporary religious communities, traditional and nontraditional. And we must remain abreast of the work being done in the area of transpersonal psychology, developing a critical interpretive method for bringing to focus the significant contents of their results while so far as possible freeing those contents from dualistic or mentalistic prejudices, naive metaphysics, and the various personal defensive systems in which they are often embedded.

In the context of this sort of empirical study of religious experience and related phenomena, we need to return to the traditional materials, Hindu, Buddhist, Sufi (to the extent that Sufism can be found in texts at all), Christian and the others. Both a fuller use of the insights of contemporary phenomenology, psychology and hermeneutics and the greatly broadened sense of the possible and familiar in experience which the empirical studies can provide should considerably enhance our interpretive resources for the explication of these materials.

Anagarika Govinda, Herbert Guenther, and Chogyam Trungpa, each in his own way, articulate in their writings a psychological-existential interpretation of Tibetan Buddhist materials. Goleman reflects on the psychology of the Abhidharma. Ornstein combines western psychology and Sufi wisdom.

These are but a few examples of the relevant sorts of fresh approach to the explication of the experiential content of the traditional accounts of religious experience. What I envision here is in a sense a new and global project of demythologizing, but one in which the interpretive preunderstanding is psychological as well as existential; one which does not exclude or delimit transcendence from the outset; one in which the capacity of the text to call the interpreter into question is more clearly and sharply recognized than Bultmann's original demythologizing project acknowledged. One central point here is the recognition at every step that the text may mediate a *disclosure* and not merely an *interpretation*.

This project for a return to the texts differs in significant respects from the program of Huston Smith and the primordialists, while sharing with them the conviction that the texts are about something and that we have by and large forgotten what it was. As I understand the primordialists, they regard the traditional texts of the great religions as conveying metaphysical truth, authentic doctrine, the substance of which is everywhere the same and is, in principle, already known to the primordialists themselves, though largely overlooked by the rest of us. I consider the question of the degree of unity of the traditions to be not only in doubt, but essentially a secondary question: a possible outcome but neither an interpretive principle nor a primary hypothesis to be tested. I believe in the potential unity of the world those texts are part of, and expect an adequate interpretation will disclose rather than conceal that unity of the world. But I do not expect that unity to be expressed in metaphysical agreement (though from time to time it may be). My basic difficulty with the primordialists, though, is that I do not regard metaphysical doctrine as the essence of religious disclosure. Metaphysics, so far as it is a worthwhile activity, consists in a reflective generalization concerning the reality-character of our experience. Ancient texts do not, I believe, function to tell us that the world is not as we experience it, something like a school teacher telling us that the world is not really flat. Ancient texts tell us of the experiences of some of our fellow-humans (including the names and characters of the numinous ones they encountered). Understanding those texts, we understand a little more the range and the context of human experience, and we open up a recognition of new possibilities for our own experience, and for (sometimes radical) revision of our fundamental sense of who we are and of what there is. Texts modify our experience of reality, rather than mediate right answers to correct our wrong ones.

In all these inquiries, our method must be phenomenological. That means at the least that we hold to a minimum our preconceptions about what the experience, or the text, will show, or how it will be interpreted. It requires excluding metaphysical prejudgments. It precludes the presumption of a Cartesian dualism of the individual thinking subject and a mathematically extended world, but it equally precludes presupposing mentalism, or the spiritual bankruptcy of materialism, or the instrumental character of the body, or the survivability of death. As carefully and patiently as we can, we must suspend judgment on all these matters and examine what shows itself. We need to take cognizance of the phenomenological analyses of human existence that have already been carried out, by Heidegger, by Sartre, by Merleau-Ponty, by Ricoeur, and others, as well as the psychological work of Freud, Jung, Reich, Rank, and the rest. Those materials we take into the study with us, to help frame questions and expose possibilities. But we do not know whether we will bring them back out, or whether the text under study, or the experience being invoked, will alter those previous results beyond recovery.

The preceding observations already note that the inquiry in question is not only a phenomenological but a hermeneutical one. It involves all the questions that are always present in the interpretation of a text. Not only explicit questions are brought to a text, but the whole body of tradition, of archetypal images, linguistic preconceptions, cultural patterns and personal motivations and defenses which participate in every act of interpretation. When we are interpreting the texts of religious experiences, it appears to me that the basic existential issues of hermeneutics are crucial. I do not mean primarily the explicit questions of existentialist philosophy. I mean rather to make the fundamental point that interpretation is an act of my being, and its possibility is predicated on the openness of my being to disclosure, to fellow-humanity, to transcendence, to the void. The challenge of a text is always at bottom this challenge, but in the texts of religious experience this challenge is at the center of the whole interpretive project precisely because these are the very issues about which the text speaks explicitly. Any major religious text calls the very selfhood, reality, meaning, and value of the interpreter into question. To the extent that we cannot bear to be thus radically questioned, we cannot understand the text.

Here, as throughout, I have laid stress on the existential factor in the proposed science. To underscore the point that methodology may not protect us from existential risk, and must not be overloaded with that extraneous burden, I wish my concluding reflections to summarize this dimension, as well as the methodological. We must accept the possibility that the domain under study is sufficiently different from our preconceptions so that it calls in question the security of our credentials. The paradigm of autonomous understanding will be brought severely into challenge, and our evasion of finitude and fallibility through methodological impersonality can only make the understanding we seek impossible. What we do experience may not mean what we are convinced it means. We must let ourselves be caught in the conflict between understanding the other's experience as my own possibility, on the one hand, and respecting the contingent particularity the other finds intrinsic to the experience. As such we seek to understand only as those who misunderstand. We must pursue methods that involve psychological and spiritual risks for those who use them. We must combine our openness and objectivity with the necessary commitments and self-discipline to qualify us to lead others into those risks, and must share the risks fully ourselves. We cannot understand texts unless we open ourselves to disclosure from the texts, which may redefine and reinterpret us more comprehensively than we can ever identify in advance.

Clearly the proposed science of religion can not be a merely materialistic and quantitative study. Direct personal experience, critical assessment of experiential reports of our contemporaries—both those who have independently entered these regions and those who may participate with us in guided explorations; both those who are following the traditional paths and those who are exploring unmarked frontiers—and a new approach to the old texts are all essential. The method involved includes centrally an element of self-study, of personal exploration. In the context of personal exploration, it also requires disciplined phenomenological clarity and restraint, and clear recognition of the depth and centrality of the hermeneutical difficulties attendant both on the quest for a fusion of horizons and on the need for a central and unlimited openness. We may hesitate to undertake such an inquiry, for we can not avoid ourselves being called into question in the course of it—it must be at once an investigation and a quest. Yet there remains an inquiry to be undertaken, and evidence and testimony to bear on it. It is time we were about it.

NOTE

/1/   I have not yet discovered in the literature any cases of lasting psychological disturbance resulting from sensory isolation in a Lilly-type chamber. This does not obviate the need for the sorts of caution already noted, but it does make this a relatively attractive mode of investigation.

WORKS CONSULTED

Barth, Karl
    1936   *Doctrine of the Word of God.* Trans. B. T. Thomson. Edinburgh: T. & T. Clark. (*Church Dogmatics,* v. 1, pt. 1.)
Bultmann, Rudolf
    1960   *Jesus Christ and Mythology.* London: SCM Press.

Crownfield, David
1976   "Religion in the Cartography of the Unconscious." *Journal of
               the American Academy of Religion* 44:309–15.
1979   "The Self Beyond Itself: Hermeneutics and Transpersonal
               Experience." *Journal of the American Academy of Religion*
               47:245–67.

Emmet, Dorothy
1945   *The Nature of Metaphysical Thinking.* London: Macmillan.

Feuerbach, Ludwig
1957   *The Essence of Christianity.* Trans. George Eliot. New York:
               Harper.

Gadamer, Hans-Georg
1975   *Truth and Method.* New York: Seabury.

Goleman, Daniel
1977   *The Varieties of Meditative Experience.* New York: Dutton.

Govinda, Anagarika
1969a   *Foundations of Tibetan Mysticism.* London: Rider.
1969b   *The Psychological Attitude of Early Buddhist Philosophy.*
               London: Rider.

Grof, Stanislav
1976   *Realms of the Human Unconscious.* New York: Dutton.
1977   *The Human Encounter With Death.* New York: Dutton. Joan
               Halifax, co-author.
1980   *Beyond Death: The Gates of Consciousness.* London: Thames
               and Hudson. Christina Grof, co-author.

Guenther, Herbert V.
1976   *The Tantric View of Life.* Boulder and London: Shambhala.

Houston, Jean, and R. L. Masters
1972   "Experimental Induction of Religious-type Experiences." In
               White, John, comp., *The Highest State of Consciousness*, pp.
               303–30. New York: Doubleday.

Huxley, Aldous
1954   *The Doors of Perception.* New York: Harper.

Ihde, Don
1980   "Interpreting Hermeneutics: Origins, Developments, and Pros-
               pects." *Man and World* 13:325–43.

James, William
1963   *The Varieties of Religious Experience.* New Hyde Park, NY:
               University Books.

Jung, Carl
1968   *Aion: Researches Into the Phenomenology of the Self.* 2nd ed.
               Trans. R.F.C. Hull. Princeton: Princeton University Press
               (Collected Works, v.9, pt.2; Bollinger Series XX).

Larson, Gerald J.
1978   "Prolegomenon to a Theory of Religion." *Journal of the American Academy of Religion* 46:443–64.

Lilly, John C.
1972   *The Center of the Cyclone.* New York: Bantam Books.
1977   *The Deep Self: Profound Isolation and the Tank Experience.* New York: Simon and Schuster. Antionette Lilly, co-author.

Monroe, Robert A.
1971   *Journeys Out of the Body.* Garden City, NY: Doubleday.

Moody, Raymond A.
1976   *Life After Life: Investigation of a Phenomenon—The Survival of Bodily Death.* Harrisburg, PA: Stackpole Books.

Ornstein, Robert
1976   *The Mind Field: A Personal Essay.* New York: Grossman Publishers.

Otto, Rudolf
1926   *The Idea of the Holy.* Trans. John W. Harvey. London: Oxford University Press.

Pahnke, Walter and Richards, W.A.
1966   "Implications of LSD and Experimental Mysticism." *Journal of Religion and Health* 5:175–208.

Pempel, Alice McDowell
1978   *Altered States of Consciousness and Mystical Experience: An Anatomy of Inner Space.* Unpublished dissertation, Fordham University.

Ring, Kenneth
1980   *Life At Death: A Scientific Investigation of the Near-Death Experience.* New York: Coward, McCann & Geoghegan.

Sanders, Ed
1977   *The Party: A Chronological Perspective on a Confrontation at a Buddhist Seminary.* Woodstock, NY: Poetry, Crime and Culture Press.

Smith, Huston
1976   *Forgotten Truth: The Primordial Tradition.* New York: Harper and Row.

Trungpa, Chögyam
1976   *The Myth of Freedom and the Way of Meditation.* Berkeley: Shambhala.

Zaehner, Robert C.
1961   *Mysticism, Sacred and Profane.* Oxford: Oxford University Press.

Three Types of Reasoning in Religion

Peter Slater

The starting point for this paper is a conviction that, in the philosophy of religion, informal considerations play a larger part in the shaping of formal arguments than some may recognize. For each type of argument there is often an unexamined, frequently unnoticed, hidden agenda guiding the framing of questions and the assessing of answers. From cross-cultural studies we may take the term 'mythos' to refer to such hidden agendas, in contrast with the term 'logos', used to refer to articulated reasoning in religion. By "mythos" is meant the whole complex of myths, symbols, and "root" metaphors from which we abstract the basic premises of our formal arguments. Such a complex is typically implicit, where "logos" is explicit, in the patterns of thought enunciated by exponents of a partucular culture or arbiters of a particular intellectual discipline. Its "hidden agenda" is embedded in the "common sense" to which they intuitively or openly appeal and without which no arguments would be possible. (See on this subject Panikkar, 1979:100, and Meland, 1976:102–9.) The apparent absence of such common ground for contemporary philosophers of religion, incidentally, may be one reason why their work often seems beside the point to serious students of religion.

In fact, there is a common ground for philosophy of religion, to be found in the nature of religion. But this has been obscured by preoccupation among western philosophers of religion with strictly theological concepts, taken out of their soteriological contexts. For the most part, western students cut their teeth on proofs for the "existence" of God, for instance, while remaining ignorant of the settings in which "gods" and "goddesses" normally appear. This ignorance is compounded by disparagement of mythological thought patterns among western philosophers, noted by such students of Indian thought as Heinrich Zimmer (1946:12, 217–21) and Mircea Eliade (1968:72–73). Western scholars too often are taught that all stories are "merely" stories, translatable without conceptual loss into abstract schemes. These latter may lack the emotive or affective tone of narrative, but supposedly omit nothing factually significant. Consequently, truth is often assumed to be a property of abstractable cognitions and arguments are supposed to proceed in lineal order from one inference to the next. In the process, logic becomes the master, not the servant, of mythic insight and the language used is increasingly removed from its religious reference range. It is no wonder that, to many, such language seems always to be "on holiday" or locked into the archaic forms of abandoned traditions.

Those of us who grew up on Wittgenstein learned that terms have meaning only in context. We no longer find acceptable analyses of single words such as 'God' or 'faith'. But it is equally unacceptable simply to focus on rules for the use of such terms in single sentences. We must consider the contexts of sentences as well. Where Wittgenstein talked of "language games" with reference to these contexts, I consider it more appropriate to religion to speak of stories. Religion as such, however, is neither a game nor a kind of story but a "form of life." (See Slater, 1978a:185, n.4.) About such forms of life it is tempting to suppose that what can be said hovers always on the "edge" of what cannot be said, that what lies "beyond" the regions susceptible to logical mapping is a "mystical" horizon. We may recognize, concerning religious discourse, that "clarity is not enough." But we still tend to assume that ever more clarification, through self-conscious criticism of unilinear entailments, is the primary objective in philosophy.

My counter-claim is not that faith is alogical or religion arational, but that the process of reasoning in religion is a dialectical one. In this process, not only does "symbol give rise to thought" but also creeds become symbols. As previous mythic patterns of argument give way to logical analyses, these analyses in turn acquire mythic force. In short, truth in religion requires us to reject the static bifurcation endorsed by the logical/mystical contrast and to acknowledge the constant interplay between articulated faith and hidden assumptions, where each new articulation buries another set of assumptions and so on. What cannot be stated is thus not some reality hidden beyond the horizon of thought, but the unacknowledged "presence" which accounts for the particular shape of each successive thought form and its changing patterns, especially in religion.

In what follows I shall review three patterns of reasoning in religion, which for convenience we shall call the analytical, the jurisprudential, and the teleological. All three are "dialectical" in some sense, but the last is most explicitly so, in ways to be considered. I shall generally presuppose familiarity with classic patterns of the first type, referring readers to examples readily available in the literature. I shall refer to contemporary work by Van Harvey and David Kelsey to illustrate the second type. But the major emphasis will be on the third type, exemplified by current accounts of "hermeneutics," notably Paul Ricoeur's interpretation of Freud and Hegel. My interest is not in formalizing the different patterns of reasoning but in what James Hillman calls "seeing through" their logical enunciation to their "mythic" presuppositions. He assumes that "the essence of consciousness is fantasy images" (1977:138–9). To the extent that he is right, any and every logical development of thought functions on the level of "explanation," certainly. But it also expresses a "depth" of meaning which equally demands understanding. Its "soul" as well as its conceptual structure calls for interpretation. In particular, for religious studies, its soteriological thrust needs to be articulated and critically examined, not only by psychologists and cultural anthropologists, but also by philosophers of religion.

1. The Analytical Type

A familiar example of the "analytical" type in philosophies of religion is the kind of deductive reasoning brought to bear on the question of evil. This question arises with respect to all traditions. The form found in most textbooks on the philosophy of religion was used, for instance, by early Buddhist critics of brahmanic Hinduism (O'Flaherty, 1976:5). The question "Why evil?" has as many answers as there are religious movements. What interests us is the set of presuppositions involved in any given framing of the question, which in turn determines the range of acceptable answers for subsequent discussion. We shall consider some standard western perspectives on this subject, brought together in a recent anthology (Urban and Walton, 1978). It begins with J. L. Mackie's statement of "the paradox of omnipotence" for "orthodox" theologians.

The paradox of omnipotence follows from this question: Can an omnipotent deity limit its own power? If not, then the "free will" defense, for instance, is of little force. The key term here is not 'power' but 'can'. For answers to questions about omnipotence hinge on *what we imagine to be possible* in this or some other world. Some writers take seriously a "utopian" thesis, while others do not. Utopian theses generally assert that there is nothing necessary about the existence of specific evils. Hence there is no contradiction in imagining our world minus these evils. Utopia is both possible and the only world an omnipotent deity should create.

Contrary opinions build on what may be called a "systems" approach which refines our notions of necessity and contradiction. John Hick, for example, contends that, although utopia may logically be something God *could* create, it is psychologically impossible, given God's intention to win the love of willful creatures (Hick, 1966:307–8). It is therefore not what God *should* create. We cannot arbitrarily modify parts of God's system, in the course of our arguments, without destroying the nature of the whole. What can and cannot, or should and should not, be expected of divine power is thus made to depend on a metaphysical, rather than a logical necessity, implicit in the very nature of purposive beings.

Concerning what is possible for divine power there is a further division of opinion. Some, like Aquinas, assert that what is logically impossible cannot be predicated of any agent, even God. Others, like Descartes, maintain that our ideas of logical possibility are limited by the finitude of our imaginations. We cannot absolutely say what is or is not possible with God (Urban & Walton:37–46). In short, for some the universe of discourse within which the laws of logic apply includes "God." For others this universe and these laws have only a limited hypothetical status. For instance, Descartes remarked that he himself could not conceive of the possibility that one plus two might not make three. But he could not *know* this conclusion to be true for all possible cases. What is possible extends beyond our capacity to think and say what God might do. We may know that God is the author of creation, and yet be unable fully to conceive or comprehend this. Much argument on the question of evil hinges on the extent to which different thinkers regard conceptualizing as a prerequisite for knowing in this context.

To the extent that Descartes is right, deductive reasoning in religion tells us more about our own limited powers of imagination than about God's omnipotence or Nirguna Brahman. Our reasoning might be formally correct in every detail, and yet its application be in error. How do we know whether our reasoning applies? Those who claim to know often simply assume that the universe is how they imagine it to be, that what cannot be conceptualized cannot be meaningfully asserted and cannot be known in any sense. But at least some analytically trained philosophers of religion are prepared to challenge this assumption. (See Immerman, 1979.) The interesting question for us is why such an assumption seems so evident to those who insist that the laws of thought have universal validity. What hidden agenda guides their choice of paradigms and makes them believe that their conclusions are somehow exempt from the astigmatism of their times?

My own suggestion, very briefly, is that those who argue deductively about evil and omnipotence, or in classical terms about the "existence" of God, tacitly assume that eternity is bound. Their hidden image of perfection is a circle, within which everything has its place. The ultimate good is synonymous with order./1/ Form is supreme, while infinite "matter" is of no account. Worse, it may be polluting./2/ According to the underlying myth of completion—the story of how, in the times before "time," things "really are"—formal logic symbolizes the most perfect kind of argument. It comes closest in fact to the "mind" of God and is our surest guide to truth. Yet ironically, as we see already in Plato, this hidden assumption can only be sustained in conjunction with a myth, that of creation by a Demiourgos (Timaeus:28–29). Concerning this it is important to notice that the story of the Demiourgos is not an expression of Plato's underlying "mythos," in the sense mentioned above. *This explicit myth hides the presence of an implicit mythos*, that of the reality of eternal truth advanced in the theory of Forms. That alone holds out to us a hint of ultimate bliss. What the theory leaves unexplained is why there should be any "moving image of eternity" for mortal cave dwellers to see or "see through." At the very heart of the theory is a surd unaccounted for by the theory, expressible only in mythological terms.

Similarly, the explicit denial of imagination, in the name of abstract insight, hides the force of such controlling images in Platonic philosophies as the Sun, the mirror, the circle, and uninterrupted space. These carry the stories establishing the "plausibility structures" by reference to which sensation is made to seem less reliable than ratiocination, principles made prior to personal judgment, and so on. What is hidden, in short, is the *blinding* effect of the "pure light" of reason, which admirably displays the figures consciously put forward for thought, but not the grounds without which they could not be seen at all.

That something is hidden by formal patterns of deductive thought is evident from the fact that other, equally profound thinkers through the ages find different truths by the light of "reason." There is no ideology to end ideology, no "once upon a time" of truth-telling concerning God and evil, which escapes the fictive aspect of mythology. For the realities in question are multifaceted, while our accounts of them are not. Certainly networks of structures undergird the regularities which our laws formulate. But how we correlate these networks depends upon the interests behind such correlations. In this connection, unilineal thinking is not wrong. Deductive reasoning remains important for theological philosophizing. But it is wrong to suppose that this reasoning alone gives us the whole truth, or even the whole picture of our rational thought-processes. It is misplaced absoluteness concerning this pattern of reasoning, not the type of reasoning as such, which makes suspect many instances of deductive reasoning in the philosophy of religion. Even if ultimate bliss is contemplation of eternity for all eternity, as many have supposed, articulation of this vision has traded on an ineradicably mythic dimension of philosophic thought. As we shall see, the other two types of reasoning are an improvement on the classical heritage in this respect. Their exponents have built into their procedures recognition of the role of paradigmatic images, *as well as* of the power of critical analysis, in religious thinking. They are more explicitly aware of their dialectical structure and thus less blinded by a show of reasoning.

Without analysis, our thinking slips all too easily into plausible nonsense. Contradictions are contradictions, no matter how sincerely uttered. But paradoxes are not contradictions. They are pointers rather to conflicts between contrasting chains of inferences. Mackie's paradox, for instance, trades on the image of a sovereign person issuing temporal orders, coupled with an ideal of perfection as unchanging, eternal, simple (not complex), impassible and so on. Given such conceptions of time and eternity, religious insight into the personal/impersonal aspects of reality cannot but be articulated in paradoxical terms./3/ To the extent that the classical arguments leave unresolved the question how "eternity" relates to "time," they never do justice to the incarnational experience permeating much theology. Critics of theology who ignore the dialectical complexities of their own premises are suspect, because they tend to leave their own comparable positions uncriticized. Their conceptions of reality rest on a surd which may in fact be an absurd basis for thinking in and of religion.

2. The Jurisprudential Type

A second type of reasoning in religion, closer to the concerns of religious life than metaphysical thought, is what we may call the jurisprudential. That this type is common should not be surprising, given that all traditions accord a major role to sacred law. The Torah, the Shari'a, the Dharma/Dhamma, Canon Law, even some interpretations of the Tao, are examples. For present purposes I shall concentrate on a contemporary discussion of Christian interpretations of scripture, which develops Stephen Toulmin's model for jurisprudential arguments (Toulmin, 1958). This model was most notably endorsed and adopted by Van Harvey, in *The Historian and the Believer* (1966). It has been systematically developed by David Kelsey in *The Uses of Scripture in Recent Theology* (1975). Before reviewing these accounts of arguments in theology, we should note that the basic pattern is not original with Toulmin. It echoes classical conceptions of rhetoric assumed by canonical authors such as Paul. (See Betz, 1979:14–25.)

Interested in "informal" or nondeductive ways of reasoning to conclusions (C) in science, ethics and the law, Toulmin differentiates among data, warrants, backing, qualifiers, rebuttals and conclusions. Often only tacitly invoked, warrants (W) are subject to qualifiers (Q) and rebuttals (R), if there is a dispute. If the warrant is challenged, backing (B) must be provided, and the whole argument becomes more complex. When the conclusion is, "Jesus was raised from the dead," the range of relevant considerations extends well beyond the norms of any one set of cultural and religious beliefs. Harvey and Kelsey believe that Toulmin's conceptions can help us to unravel this kind of conclusion.

Where Harvey's preoccupation is primarily with the justification of theological interpretations of history, Kelsey's account is of how theologians actually appeal to scripture (not what they theorize about its authority). According to Kelsey, none of seven different Protestants, including Tillich and Barth, directly deduces theological conclusions from scriptural statements (1975:185–94). Scripture is not simply "translated" into theological formulations. The arguments of all such theologians involve a complex blending of considerations—from history, the phenomenology of religion, metaphysics, and biblical exegesis. No single statement, or set of statements, constitutes a sufficient warrant for any single conclusion. In an "informal" argument, data, warrants, qualifiers, and rebuttals, all combine to form a *pattern* of judgments, from which a given conclusion is derived. Moreover, what in one part of an argument is the warrant becomes, if challenged, the datum for another argument. We cannot tell from the form or source of a statement, taken in isolation, what role it plays in any given dispute. Only in context do we see how it fits into an overall pattern.

An example from Kelsey in the Toulmin format is as follows (1975:130–33):

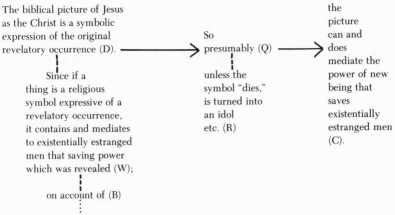

a phenomenology of religious experiences of revelatory occurrences, taking the disciples' encounter with Jesus as the paradigm instance.

That such arguments invoke metaphysical assertions is shown by Kelsey with reference to Barth, whose interpretation of revelation depends on a particular conception of personal agency.

Kelsey emphasizes the fact that no single type of datum, warrant, or backing—in particular, no authoritative quotation from scripture—can be a sufficient reason for accepting a given conclusion. Harvey agrees but stresses the obverse point, that historically warranted data form a necessary, though not sufficient, ingredient in Christian theologizing about Jesus. (See also Harvey, 1979.) Harvey inquires into the morality of reaching "hard" conclusions on the basis of "soft" data. Kelsey reminds us of the multiplicity of considerations implicitly or explicitly adduced in all theological arguments. But both speak less and less of logical inferences, and more and more of imaginative judgments, when describing how historically minded theologians actually arrive at their conclusions.

Neither Harvey nor Kelsey gives us much insight into how Christian theologians arrive at the perspectives which shape their final judgments. In a recent essay, Kelsey makes clear that the "givens" of religious reasoning are tied, in an "active" tradition, to its use of scripture (1980:393–401). But the tradition's norms and criteria are not "systematizable." The set of focal images, parables, metaphors, action-guides and the like given in the use of biblical literature as "scripture" is so heterogeneous that independent judgment must be exercised (1980:398). Similarly, Harvey acknowledges that "all of our thinking and knowing rests on acritical beliefs, on what [Michael Polanyi] calls a fiduciary framework" (1979:408). Harvey endorses the view that we begin by believing and must have grounds for doubting. There is no "universal imperative not to believe anything on insufficient evidence" (412). But there are "role-specific" obligations to resolve reasonable doubts, in relation to which we may speak of a "right to believe" (413). In such contexts, we inquire into the authority, evidence, and procedures used for testing specific claims (415). Harvey does not specify the roles relevant for theology but again invokes Toulmin for an account of the kind of reasoning involved. The hidden ideal here is no longer that of theoretical forms, to be followed necessarily, but that of a perfect judge, on whose authoritative imagination we somewhat arbitrarily depend.

Following Robert C. Johnson, Kelsey maintains that at work in Christian thinking is a "discrimen," or configuration, of organically related criteria concerning the canon of scripture and the nature of ultimate reality. This provides a paradigmatic set of images which governs a theologian's emphases in matters of faith and practice: "at the root of a theological position there is an imaginative act in which a theologian tries to catch up in a single metaphorical judgment the full complexity of God's presence in, through, and over-against the activities comprising the church's common life and which, in turn, both provides the *discrimen* against which theology criticizes the church's current forms of speech and life, and determines the peculiar 'shape' of the 'position'" (1975:163). The ideal judge weighs factors to arrive at a holistic conclusion about Christian identity in community, which is prior to any particular articulation of data, warrants, and backing.

According to Kelsey, each theologian *can* produce arguments for his or her position, given prior decisions as a member of a religious community and participant in the wider culture. But nothing requires that the pivotal act of "imaginative judgment" must itself "have been arrived at through a reasoned argument" (1975:171). This vital judgment generates the metaphors and analogies articulating each theologian's construal of the *discrimen*, the "horizontal" constraints of tradition and the "vertical" sense of God's "presence" (178, n.6). Formally, the pattern imposed may lead deductively from scripture, as "perfect source," to what supposedly is implicit in the text (194). But the authoritative force of scripture is akin to that of law, which is only normative "to the extent that it can be elaborated to meet unforeseen developments and to cover novel legal problems" (195). Both reasoning and imagination are at work here. But it is an imaginative "vision" of what Christianity is "all about" that provides the "whole," within which reasoned argument takes place (177, 206). The articulation of such a vision, I submit, is intrinsically mythological.

Similarly, Harvey's resolution of questions of faith and history builds on a conception of paradigmatic events and contrasting perspectives. He focuses on the "gestalt" formed by a "perspectival image" of Jesus, which is based on the "memory-impressions" communicated by the New Testament. "Jesus Christ is the key image in a parable which the Christian uses to interpret the more inclusive reality with which all men are confronted and of which they try to make some sense" (1966:283; note also 273). But the precise configuration of memory-impressions is different for different schools of thought. Harvey particularly differentiates his conception of Jesus from what he calls "the Biblical Christ" of the Fourth Gospel (281). Here the hidden agenda of his own perspective emerges, as he looks for a sense in which the Jesus story can be true according to the canons of modern secular knowledge. Granting that faith is presupposed in the articulation of any perspective, he denies that Christian faith must necessarily violate these canons (281–89). His discussion ends where Kelsey's begins, with recognition that scriptural material is part, but not the whole, of any authoritative pattern of Christian faith.

Harvey's predilection is clearly to give logical reasoning pride of place in any community of civilized people. (See 1979:417.) "Mythological" means to him "factually untrue" (1966:280, also 197, 233). Myth may have mediated faith in the past. But for "modern men" the "call to faith" among Christians is "more powerful. . .if interpreted in terms of the (demythologized) memory-image of Jesus" (281). Yet, alluding to Buber's concept of *Sage*, Harvey also writes approvingly of the "mythologization" of history, construing 'myth' then to mean not "a false story but a highly selective story that is used to structure and convey the basic self-understanding of a person or a community. A pattern is abstracted from [a paradigmatic] event and becomes the formalized parable that is used to interpret larger tracts of history and experience" (257). This way of speaking is tied to a description of religions as, among other things, "symbolic forms" for interpreting fundamental aspects of being, "in the light of a certain basic concern for beatitude and fulfillment" (264). There is no religious perspective as such, Harvey contends, but a family of resembling orientations, each expressing and prescribing slightly different priorities with regard to the whole of life (1966:261–62; 1979:418).

Two conclusions from these adaptations of Toulmin's model are important for our topic. The first is that religious reasoning occurs in the context of image-driven faith. In order to describe this process we must speak in terms of symbols, emblems, paradigms, stories, myths, parables, models, and so on. There is no privileged plane of metaphysical or logical discourse, in relation to which symbols and stories are mere illustrations of independently formulated truth. Those who dismiss stories as such remain oblivious to the "mythos" on which their own use of "logos" rests. Even the best minds among interpreters of our western traditions demonstrate the inescapable appeal to key images, implicitly or explicitly, in religious arguments.

The second point pertains to what orients our faith. Here Harvey's concluding discussion is revealing. For he clearly states that religious interest is in our present *and future*. The concern is with "beatitude" and "fulfillment" (1966:264). What religion in fact involves us in, so to speak, is a "politics of the spirit" dealing not only in eternal verities and historic events, but also in the rational shaping of interests, aspirations, hopes, expectations, and life-fulfilling realizations of existential truth. Both Harvey (1979:420) and Kelsey (1980:386) recognize this point. Yet the models of reasoning so far advanced, if no longer atemporal and mathematical in inspiration, have been primarily legal and historical. The ideal implicit in the jurisprudential type of reasoning is shaped by a myth of final judgment based on evidence that in principle is already in. The orientation is to the past, even though the application of "the Law" may be to the present and future. At least as developed so far, the analytical and jurisprudential types do not allow us to do justice to the eschatological thrust or teleological counterweight to claims of tradition in religious reasoning. To this kind of dialectic we turn our attention next.

3. The Teleological Type

What Harvey and Kelsey demonstrate, among other things, is that, in traditions like Christianity, there is no absolute datum from which we simply read off all necessary conclusions for our way of life. Religious truth is not already somehow given, if only implicitly, so that our sole task is to make explicit what in principle is unalterably "the case." Instead, the suggestion seems to be that we scan a range of necessary, but individually insufficient ingredients of a given decision, focus on a "root metaphor" or "paradigmatic event," apply formal and informal reasoning to our data, and then sum up the whole process in an imaginative act of judgment. As a description of religious thinking this is an improvement on old-style deductivism. But it makes too little of the eschatological interest in religious life and leaves in doubt the rationality of the starting-point. Reason here remains "the slave of the passions." By acknowledging more than one possible starting-point, the jurisprudential model allows for a change in our choice of warrants or backing. But as long as reasoning does not enter into the initial faith perspective, the rationality of the whole procedure seems in jeopardy.

That there may be good and sufficient reasons, but not the stated reasons, underlying image-driven faith is readily suggested by any study of Feuerbach or Freud. Let us consider in this connection Paul Ricoeur's masterly study of Freud, not for what it teaches about Freud, but for the conclusions reached by Ricoeur himself. He comes to mind because of his detailed analysis of the role of symbols in religious thought. His earlier conception of this was less dialectical. "Symbols give rise to thought," he reminded us, but not that creeds and political manifestoes become symbols. Recently, he has emphasized metaphors instead. His interest throughout has been in evoking a sense of double meaning, such as Freud discerns in dreams (Ricoeur, 1970:5–7). What emerges, however, is not only a sense of double meaning but also delineation of a *double movement*, between past and future, the hidden and the revealed, which characterizes any dialectical model. It is not metaphor as such, or the literal as such, which is significant, but the reversal of expectations effected by the use of *either* metaphor *or* literal discourse. (See Slater, 1978b:305.) This is true especially for a biblical conception of parables, of which Ricoeur has become a leading exponent (1975).

With the gift of hindsight, we may notice in passing that Harvey (1966) used the terms 'myth' and 'parable' more or less interchangeably. In recent years, some New Testament critics have argued for technical distinctions between these terms, suggesting that, whereas myths tend to reaffirm the cosmic *status quo* in a given culture, parables serve to undermine it. Jesus' Parable of the Good Samaritan, for instance (Luke 10:29–37), calls in question the entire Temple mythology of pre-Rabbinic or late Israelite religion. When shorn of subsequent allegorical moralizing, parables typically end with existential questions. Jesus' parables reverse his hearers' priorities and reform their expectations concerning the coming of God's kingdom. Parables presuppose myths but transfigure their meaning (Crossan, 1975:48–60). This account of their kerygmatic purpose may be unduly existentialist. Our point does not rest on its terminology or details of biblical interpretation. We could as well speak of myth, anti-myth and counter-myth, in the interplay of religious thought. (See Smith, 1978 and O'Flaherty, 1980.) Whatever language is used, and however we interpret particular stories, the general conclusion is clear, that religious thought proceeds by the juxtaposing of images in stories and through patterns of argument which relate past to future, in ways which transform the present.

Keeping in mind this general conclusion, let us consider Ricoeur's study of Freud. Like Nietzsche and Marx, Ricoeur comments, Freud practises a "hermeneutics of suspicion" rather than a "hermeneutics of recollection" of meaning (1970:32–36). This emphasis on hermeneutics, accepted and extended by Ricoeur, exemplifies one aspect of what has been called "the linguistic turn" in modern philosophy. On this subject, we do well to heed Richard Rorty's contrast between hermeneutics and epistemology. Whereas epistemologists look for the "foundations" of all thought in commensurable discourse, taking as normal an agreement in principle about what *might* be meant, hermeneuticists struggle to comprehend what, according to the dictates of any ruling paradigm, seems *abnormal*. Hermeneutics "is not the name for a distinctive discipline but a plea for openness" against the constraints of prevailing epistemologies (Rorty, 1979:315–16). It is not the kind of justificatory enterprise insisted on by Harvey, as earlier by Freud, to the extent that the latter regarded himself as a "guardian of rationality" (317). If we follow Rorty, we shall not allow either philosopher or psychiatrist to be king, but call on both to be hermeneutic partners in an open-ended conversation concerning relative meanings. This indeed is what Ricoeur seeks with Hegel and Freud.

Ricoeur first analyses Freud's "economics of desire" in its own terms, as an "archeological" enterprise. But he breaks through its prescriptive and restrictive aspects to relate its findings concerning double meaning to Hegel's teleological philosophy. Implicit in the discussion of the origins of motivation he finds a dialectic of consciousness, particularly in Freud's remarks concerning identification and sublimation. The term 'dialectic' here points to more that the presence of a dichotomy—between archeology and teleology, conscious and unconscious, sacred and profane, centers and margins, normal and abnormal, or any other pair. It points to *the coimplication of one term by the other*. For religious thought, it reminds us especially of the interplay of immanence and transcendence in any adequate conception of a saving or liberating way of life. Applied to Freud's thought by Ricoeur, it develops the teleological motifs espoused explicitly in Hegel's phenomenology, as well as the "archeological" concerns implicit in Hegel and explicit in Freud (459–98). Ricoeur insists that this juxtaposition of Freud's psychoanalysis with Hegel's phenomenology is not crass eclecticism. It genuinely opens up a different level of understanding of the data, which is neither that of analysis alone nor a contradiction of it. What Ricoeur here states concerning archeology and teleology, with reference to Freud and Hegel, seems to me applicable to any account of reasoning in religion.

One weakness of nineteenth-century dialectical thinking (noted by Rorty concerning the dichotomy of spirit and nature), was its tendency to ontologize polarities and assimilate features of one set with another. The result was a fruitless debate over realism and idealism, in search of the ultimate "arche" or foundation-point in epistemology and theories of the self. Another weakness, following from the absolutising of particular polarities, was the assumption that dialectical reasoning proceeds by identifying one, and only one, "opposite" for every postulate—*the* antithesis which will lead us from thesis to synthesis. This weakness is evident in Eliade's polarity of the sacred and the profane. For as Victor Turner (1969) and Jonathan Z. Smith (1978) remark, religious dialectic trades on chaotic and revolutionary, as well as on structuring and conservative, movements of the spirit. There are times in the history of religions, for instance, when secularity rather than religiosity constitutes "good news," so that secularity and the sacred go together. Eliade's conception is too undialectical, at least in his earliest accounts of it. Ricoeur, who often follows Eliade, is similarly tempted to stop at a conception of double meaning, without recognizing fully the double movements of religious thought. But on Freud and Hegel he explicitly emphasizes the dialectical interplay between the coimplications of archeological and teleological thinking.

In psychoanalytic thought, coimplication emerges in discussions of sexuality. The narcissism of the ego is modified by desire to be like another, to possess another and to find some alternative to the choice between ego-loss and loss of the other. The process of sublimation trades on symbolization of these inner conflicts and seeks resolution of them on the plane of culture. Ricoeur does not assess the adequacy of such Freudian conceptions. Instead he uses them to show that the question of identity is a question about symbolism, regression and progression, and that the analytic procedures of cultural archeology must be complemented by a teleological hermeneutics. Freud's significance lies in his "dispossession of consciousness as the arbiter of meaning" (1970:494). This is linked to cultural and religious demands that we transcend our egotistical pretensions to omnipotence and omniscience through ethics, aesthetics and mythology.

Symbols are a key to liberating transcendence for Ricoeur because they are polyvalent. In particular, as contrasted with dream symbols and those studied in cultural anthropology, the "prospective" symbols of religious philosophy enable us to confront the problems of false consciousness and alienation in the sphere of culture, especially on matters of valuation and worth (1970:505–9). On this point, Walter Lowe justly remarks that Ricoeur sides finally with Hegel, against Freud and Marx (Lowe, 1978:253). In a concluding *tour de force*, Ricoeur considers the revealing-concealing power of symbolism in *Oedipus Rex*, not archeologically as sexual myth but teleologically as metonym for our blindness and ultimate vision (1970:519). Within Christian theology we may supplement these insights with Moltmann's emphasis on eschatological reasoning, following Morse's explication of this as a dialectical juxtaposition of performative and descriptive uses of language (Morse, 1979:37–41, 130). The important point throughout is not some theory of symbols and double meanings, but recognition of the teleological component of religious dialectics.

What the teleological thrust to religious thinking adds to reflections on the roots of religious consciousness, as I read Ricoeur, is a better understanding of why we thematise consciousness as we do. Harvey and Kelsey, we recall, emphasized the importance of thematic patterns or paradigms in theology, without offering any compelling reasons for their centrality in religious thought. A teleological model for religious thinking, developing the dialectic of tradition and hope, explains our correlations of reason and passion, reason and revelation, gospel and law, by applying the concept of coimplication to the fundamentally soteriological concerns of religious traditions. (Consider in this context Tillich's analysis of such polarities in his *Systematic Theology*.) What is "thematised" is, in Freudian terms, the question of identification and sublimation.

Religious reasoning is reasoning about our identity and ideal destiny, creation and redemption. It is dialectical because redemption or liberation hinges on the realization of a new identity, breaking the bonds of earlier "master-slave" relationships. Coimplication here means that religious descriptions of present facts carry with them demands for transforming action. And religious promises of a new future carry with them demands that we authenticate such promises by reference to the best available knowledge of the present world (so Morse on Moltmann). The relevant morality in this context, *contra* Harvey, is not just that of historical research into the past but also that of revolutionary politics in the present. As Moltmann points out (1970:164), the role-specific obligations of secular historians are less relevant to Christian thinking than those of a truly Christian mission in the modern world. In Austinian terms, the relevant judgments are not only verdictive, but also commissive, behabitive, exercitive and expositive (Morse, 1979:70–1).

Ricoeur gives us one of the best statements to date of the dialectical nature of religious thought and the inalienably mytho-poetic component of such thought. But he himself is still too tied to a Protestant version of kerygmatic theology, in which demythologizing is *always* preferred to remythologizing. He espouses a theology of the Wholly Other which has difficulty acknowledging the "logos" side of the mythos-logos polarity, the "humanity" of divinity, if you will. Ironically, this may be because he does not sufficiently follow up his own insights concerning myths and symbols. He has shown us that these live through cycles of stories in which meanings change, as one myth becomes dominant rather than another (1967). But he has not yet explored sufficiently the "logic of promissory narration" (to use Morse's phrase), despite his recognition that the symbolism of evil is logically secondary to that of salvation. If "sin gets its full meaning only retrospectively" (1967:307), then its meaning must depend on whatever patterns our "prospective" symbols impose on our thinking, as this is shaped by eschatological imagination. These are the patterns which contemporary philosophers of religion most need to examine.

Where the other types of reasoning assumed a standpoint in eternity or orientation primarily towards the past, the teleological type emphasizes the future. Consequently, it is essential to a complete account of religious thought. By contrast with the first, the second and third types reflect an incomplete shift in what Jonathan Smith calls our "locative" sense (1978:101–3, 291–94). Our imagery of self may no longer be primarily spatial, placing ourselves or "the sacred" at the center. In Tillich's autobiographical image, we may think of ourselves as living "on the boundary." But in our talk of time, the center still tends to be present self-consciousness. Among contemporary philosophers of religion, John Hick calls for a "Copernican revolution" on this front also (1976:30–34). But the very imagery of standpoints and perspectives brings us back to an egocentric present. How can we take our stand on the margins of our own consciousness, in a time that is "not yet" for us? Hick attempts this by introducing nonwestern traditions, according to which "ego" at last finds an inclusive identity with what is more than self. But in this Hick, like Ricoeur, seems finally to subscribe to the myth of progress which undergirds most teleological thinking in western traditions.

Different traditions give different accounts of what it means to lose the old self and realize a new identity. But none of them achieves its ends by absolutizing one logical or rhetorical type to the neglect of others. In the holistic spirit of contemporary studies what we need, as Ricoeur recognizes, is not an indiscriminate eclecticism of traditions, but dialectics in the sense of genuine conversation. What is absolute is not the starting-point or end-point, nor even present consciousness, but the process itself. We may seem here to make conversation itself a false absolute. But genuine conversation destroys all pretensions to anyone's saying the last word. As Ricoeur and Rorty point out, the moral of hermeneutics for religious thought is precisely that we *cannot* evade individual responsibility, either for where we enter a conversation or for how it turns out, by invoking some higher morality or supposedly neutral authority, in support of one or other position.

The concept of coimplication as a key to dialectical thinking returns us finally to our initial contrast between explicit reasoning and hidden agendas. "Mythos," we recall, is not any particular myth or parable but the hidden story of particular patterns of myths and arguments. It includes the unstated reasons constituting the level of agreement presupposed in logic and epistemology. Dialectical thinking relativizes this agreement but the result is not utter relativism. For in any given situation, the changing set of figures shaping our thoughts extends beyond perception of this common ground to mythic visions of a new future. The reductive descriptions of our situations, required for analytic thinking, leave the horizon of present perceptions mysterious and nonrational. Their static portrayals of resurrection-talk, for instance, invite us to label this flatly true or false, instead of prompting us to unravel the soteriological implications and half-truths of traditional resurrection narratives. Dialectically developed descriptions, by contrast, allow for the fact that *part* of what was once meant may be affirmed today, while part is reconceived. (On such conceptual relativism in the sciences see Toulmin, 1972.) Dialectical descriptions direct thought beyond configurations of the moment and challenge us to transfigure our perceptions of it. Each piece of formal reasoning is only the foreground, so to speak, of a wider background which includes the possible cultures, standpoints, and perspectives inherent in the moment. It is this background which makes both argument and conversation feasible.

If examining our hidden agendas is one object of hermeneutics, and hermeneutics is conversation exploring abnormal meanings, as contrasted with received opinions, still in hermeneutics we assume that conversation has some rational point. We do not simply shoot strangers on sight. We may have no common *stated* world of discourse within which to articulate the truth of our relationships. But there is an unstated commonality in our potentially common destiny, which constrains the autonomy and heteronomy of each dialogical occasion. (See Ricoeur, 1967:167). In Tillich's terms, there is a theonomous absolute qualifying each cultural moment. (See also Rupp, 1979:58.) Recognition of this hidden presence is the *sine qua non* of all types of reasoning in western religions, whether this is imagined as infinite source, ultimate judge or power of the future. No logic alone gives us an absolute idea of its potential depths. Only through the juxtaposition of our images and inferences, in the context of changing cycles of myths and arguments, do we discern this presence, as that which both affirms the truth of the moment and drives us to transform it. What is "coimplied" in each articulation of such truth is not some utopian universe of purely logical possibilities, but a very concrete set of live options for the parties to a "conversation." In each moment, we build *to*, not *from*, a common world of discourse and rationality is realized in the dialectic of tradition and hope which informs present perspectives. To realize such rationality we must acknowledge, besides the analytic and jurisprudential types, the teleological thinking implicit in the myths of endings, as well as beginnings, of all religious traditions.

NOTES

/1/   In this connection, note the corrections to Eliade's Platonic emphasis on order in J. Z. Smith, 1978. See also the discussion of Augustine in Slater, 1981.

/2/   See Mary Douglas, 1966:2.

/3/   With reference to Kierkegaard on this subject see J. Heywood Thomas, 1957. Most critics of Kierkegaard distort his meaning by assimilating individuality to particularity and ignoring the dialectical difference between "passion" and sensation.

WORKS CONSULTED

Betz, Hans Dieter
    1979   *Galatians*. A Commentary on Paul's Letter to the Churches in
                    Galatia. Philadelphia: Fortress.

Crossan, John Dominic
    1975   *The Dark Interval: Towards A Theology of Story*. Niles, IL:
                    Argus.

Douglas, Mary
    1966   *Purity and Danger*. An analysis of the concepts of pollution
                    and taboo. London: Routledge & Kegan Paul.

Eliade, Mircea
    1968   *The Quest*. History and Meaning in Religion. Chicago: The
                    University of Chicago Press.

Harvey, Van
    1966   *The Historian and the Believer*. New York: Macmillan.

1971   "The Alienated Theologian." In *The Future of Philosophical Theology*, edited by Robert A. Evans. Philadelphia: Westminster.

1979   "The Ethics of Belief Reconsidered." *The Journal of Religion* 59.4 (October):406–20.

Hick, John
1966   *Evil and the God of Love*. London: Macmillan.
1976   *Death and Eternal Life*. London: Collins.

Hillman, James
1977   *Re-Visioning Psychology*. New York: Harper Colophon.

Immerman, Leon Andrew
1979   "Must we know what we say?" *Religious Studies* 15.3 (September):265–80.

Kelsey, David
1975   *The Uses of Scripture in Recent Theology*. Philadelphia: Fortress.
1980   "The Bible and Christian Theology." *Journal of the American Academy of Religion* 48/3 (September):403–13.

Lowe, Walter
1978   Review of Ricoeur 1970. *Religious Studies Review* 4.4 (October):246–54.

Meland, Bernard E.
1976   *Fallible Forms and Symbols*. Philadephia: Fortress.

Moltmann, Jurgen & Herzog, Frederick
1970   *The Future of Hope*. Theology as Eschatology. New York: Herder & Herder. (Includes essay by Van Harvey.)

Morse, Christopher
1979   *The Logic of Promise in Moltmann's Theology*. Philadelphia: Fortress.

O'Flaherty, Wendy Doniger
1976   *The Origins of Evil in Hindu Mythology*. Berkeley: University of California Press.
1980   "Inside and Outside the Mouth of God: The Boundary Between Myth and Reality." *Daedalus: Journal of the American Academy of Arts and Sciences*, 109.2 (Spring):93–125.

Panikkar, R.
1979   *Myth, Faith and Hermeneutics*. New York: Paulist.

Ricoeur, Paul
1967   *The Symbolism of Evil*. Trans. Emerson Buchanan. New York: Harper & Row.
1970   *Freud and Philosophy: An Essay on Interpretation*. Trans. Denis Savage. New Haven: Yale University Press.
1975   "Biblical Hermeneutics." *Semeia: An Experimental Journal for Biblical Criticism* 4:29–148.

Rorty, Richard
    1979   *Philosophy and the Mirror of Nature.* Princeton: Princeton
                    University Press.

Rupp, George
    1979   *Beyond Existentialism and Zen: Religion in a Pluralistic
                    World.* New York: Oxford University Press.

Slater, Peter
    1978a   *The Dynamics of Religion: Meaning and Change in Religious
                    Traditions.* New York: Harper & Row.
    1978b   "The Kerygma and the Cuckoo's Nest." *Scottish Journal of
                    Theology* 31.4:301–18.
    1981   "The Transcending Process and the Relocation of the Sacred."
                    In *Transcendence and the Sacred,* edited by Alan Olson.
                    Notre Dame: University of Notre Dame Press.

Smith, Jonathan Z.
    1978   *Map is Not Territory.* Leiden: E. J. Brill.

Thomas, J. Heywood
    1957   *Subjectivity and Paradox.* Oxford: Basil Blackwell.

Toulmin, Stephen
    1958   *The Uses of Argument.* Cambridge: Cambridge University
                    Press.
    1972   *Human Understanding: The Collective Use and Evolution of
                    Concepts.* Princeton: Princeton University Press.

Turner, Victor
    1969   *The Ritual Process: Structure and Anti-Structure.* Ithaca, NY:
                    Cornell University Press.

Urban, Linwood & Walton, Douglas N.
    1978   *The Power of God: Readings on Omnipotence and Evil.* New
                    York: Oxford University Press.

Zimmer, Heinrich
    1946 (1962)   *Myths and Symbols in Indian Art and Civilization.* New
                    York: Harper Torchbook.

II.
The Perplexities of Theological Endeavor

Argument in Theology:
Analogy and Narrative

David B. Burrell

Philosophers require a special sense of 'argument' which presents the initial hurdle in introducing students to the discipline. Negotiating that hurdle gives one an opportunity to reflect on the noble yet ineffectual character of philosophy, of course, for it is significant that we ordinarily associate arguments with pushing, shoving, and shouting. If philosophy promises to replace all that with reasoned discourse, the ordinary connotations offer meager evidence of success. Yet we continue to push on, drawn by the vision of a better world, to invite our students to taste the nonviolent resolution of reasoned discourse.

If we choose our examples judiciously, we can usually manage to bring a few to discover how natural are the grooves of reasoning to the human spirit, and some will even find themselves rejoicing in the beauty of a finely honed argument. Those drawn to mathematics will normally be grouped here as well, along with others whose temperament will charge them with less well-ordered tasks, but who can nonetheless appreciate the economy and grace of rigorous argument. From among these will emerge a few aspiring philosophers, charmed by reasoned discourse and lured by the hope of using it to tame those regions of human endeavor to which their spirit calls them. What follows is a story of philosophical development intertwined with personal growth—a story quite inadequately rendered in the idiom of professional advancement.

That story is shared by most of us, and it accounts for the fruitful interaction between teaching and inquiry that philosophers seem to enjoy more than most other scholars. For the ranging concerns of our students draw us yet more insistently to adapt disciplined argument to one humane endeavor after another. And so we grow as well, as philosophers and as human beings. The versions differ, and no course is normative, yet there are typical features. My own odyssey from a romance with the "great ideas" of classical writers through the rigorous initiations of symbolic logics and mathematics to philosophy of science, and then through the crucible of war resistance to philosophical theology and recurring issues of social justice, may be shared in its particulars by a few, yet it exemplifies remarkably Whitehead's pattern for learning philosophy: from romance to rigor to wider ranging concerns. Yet more significantly, however, one can recount the story as a struggle to reconcile the ideal of argument as reasoned discourse with a human concern that carries us into regions fraught with ambiguity.

To the extent that we allow ourselves to follow those concerns, we will find the territory less and less amenable to the paradigms of understanding available to us. So the struggle can be identified: relating that paradigm with these concerns so as to discover their mutual relevance, and in the process one's own integrity. The temptation to let go of either pole to release the tension by disavowing any relationship, remains ever with us. *Les hommes d'affaires* will be solicited to let concern collapse into self-interest, and reasoned discourse into calculating advantages; *les philosophes* will want to take refuge in the structures of argument for their own sake, forgetting how they themselves were initially drawn by the promise such discourse held for a fresh way of resolving misunderstandings. It was their inchoate sense for understanding itself as a human concern that drew them into philosophy over objections from within and without.

So a continuing effort to relate rational paradigm with human concern remains, I am now arguing, at the center of the philosophical task. I shall dwell no further on my personal account, but mentioned it to introduce a mode of argument which I shall be elucidating here. It involves appropriating one's own development as a living illustration of the paradigms (or criteria) at work. The gap between actual realization and ideal will set off the paradigms *as* paradigms by displaying criteria at work. And the skill with which I am able to accomplish that *showing* will call forth from each reader the evidence needed to concur or to demur, and so indicate the lacunae as well as the adequacy of my presentation. In this way the argument can advance, but only as *we* participate in it.

The weakest point doubtless lies with the skill of this one presenting, but others can contribute to such an argument's failing by persistently eschewing reflection on the way the criteria have in fact shaped their work and lives. Socrates distinguished those who sought after wisdom from those who deemed themselves wise by the willingness to let the critical edge of argument turn to foster self-awareness as well. The fact that Plato chose to display this turn in dialogues lends considerable weight to the central point of my argument. Yet that point will be highlighted or obscured by my ability to make this presentation effectively self-referential: it must not only present but carry an argument to make the point it wishes to make about argument in theology. Yet since I am constantly being made aware of the limits of my skills of presentation, I have needed to alert my readers directly that they will be invited to shift their perspective on some favorite paradigms in the course of this argument about argument./1/

Peculiarities of Argument in Theology

There was a time when philosophy of religion could claim no place in the academy. For its very subject—religion—was too obviously mired in subjectivity to offer any leverage for critical and objective clarification. The discipline could find room only in divinity schools or in colleges and universities supported by the churches. And in such locations, its practitioners were usually concerned to display those features of religious convictions and commitment which met the test of objectivity. In such a climate, philosophy of religion served as a gadfly to one's colleagues in religion, or a mode of apologetics to those more enamored of argument. That the discipline has come to occupy a fairly respectable place in departments of philosophy, if not in the wider academy, can be traced to that confluence of factors in the sixties which cast considerable shadows on conventional paradigms of objectivity.

Rather than belabor that loss of cumulative certitudes, however, I prefer to acknowledge the earlier fears about religion's link with subjectivity. Yet our considerable and growing disquietude with *objectivity* should warn us that we can no longer accept an earlier generation's characterization of *subjectivity*. For it turns out to have been a largely unexamined correlate of the very notion (of objectivity) which has not stood subsequent examination. So philosophy of religion finds itself pressed into a fresh way of characterizing its subject, and is pressed to do so by the very intellectual and cultural forces which gained it acceptance into the academy. It is unlikely that the characterization which I shall offer will be much more acceptable to the present academy, but the difficulties will no longer be proper to academe. Any invitation to move from criticism to self-criticism is likely to be declined by almost all of us—not because we are academics but merely in virtue of being human beings./2/ First, however, to some more obvious stumbling blocks.

The clarity of reasoned discourse fascinates us, not simply for aesthetic reasons but for the way it promises to resolve disputes nonviolently. The "grammatical" discovery that logic does not coerce is the beginning of philosophy and the key to the place it holds in human hopes. Yet nothing seems so impervious to logic as theological disputation, and no differences breed violence so quickly and so deeply as religious ones. *Odium theologicum* threatens any attempt at sustained discourse in faculties of divinity, and the history of Christianity is punctuated by church councils attempting to mediate dogmatic controversies only to find their formulas giving rise to fresh animosities—many of which precipitated armed conflict and even war. Any prudent philosopher would retire before a field so steeped in violence. How could rational arbitration hope to guide us across?

To the Enlightenment mind such a situation could only testify to a lesser stage in human development. Yet in the longer view one had to admit that monotheism represented a substantial advance in human culture. So why not seek beyond particularity for the enlightened core of religious belief? If one could find an appropriate rational expression for that core, then one could preserve the gains of monotheistic belief without its atavistic residue. Here we have the motivation for the search for an adequate philosophical vehicle for Christian faith which, once formulated, could express its catholic pretensions in a universal human idiom.

The process conceals an antinomy, of course, which surfaces by rendering religion irrelevant the moment it succeeds in passing such a test. For if one can adequately express a particular revelation in a universal language, then what need for its original idiom? In terms familiar since Hegel, once we can dispense with the imaginative trappings, then humankind will have advanced beyond the religious stage to that of pure reason. This popular reading of Hegel has been effectively contested by Emil Fackenheim's careful study, but the legacy remained. Fackenheim acknowledges that Hegel indeed spoke of successive stages, but that consistency with his own formulation of dialectical reasoning, and its specific virtues, demands the copresence of religious and rational expression. Human understanding progresses precisely by the interaction of particular with universal, actual instance with abstract formulation, and to remove that possibility would end all movement in thought. So despite his predilection for naming pure reason the ultimate stage in human understanding, Hegel could not admit to one achieving that term—at the price of terminating that reasoning proper to philosophical understanding: dialectic.

So the Enlightenment dream of replacing religion with reason, when closely analyzed, proves as incoherent as it in fact proved ineffectual. The twentieth century has demonstrated that religion had no monopoly on violence, and that on balance it contained within it moderating elements absent in a secular ideology. On a mere philosophical level, the search for an "adequate conceptuality" for religious faith proved self-defeating./3/ The dream of liberal Christianity to reformulate the tradition in neutral terms tantamount to monotheism evacuated religious belief of its properly transcendent character, and left humankind with no reason to worship. Fackenheim's analysis of Hegel was proven correct in fact.

That the search for *a* philosophical criterion proved vain, however, does not obviate the need for philosophical clarification. Perhaps there are several criteria, operating jointly, so as to offer one critical purchase on religious affirmations without reducing them to philosophical assertions. An approach of this sort characterized Bernard Lonergan's *Method in Theology*. While presuming an operating familiarity with his thesis, I shall highlight the factors which emerge as philosophically significant—notably his shift of center from theory to interiority.

From Theory to Interiority

Theologians in quest of method have customarily been attracted to a philosophical idiom to order their reflections appropriately. Indeed, theologies can fairly well be distinguished by the conceptual frameworks they employ to elucidate the "depth structure" of a community's life of worship and service. So we find the Greek fathers enamored of Platonism, with Augustine adopting a yet more Plotinian form. This approach carried theological reflection until Bonaventure, whose contemporaries Albert and Aquinas found themselves compelled to consider, as well as attracted by, the new philosophy of Aristotle. The unfolding of that union—known as *scholasticism*—has been marked by high points and low, challenged creatively by early renaissance figures like Nicholas of Cusa, and more polemically by the sixteenth-century reformers. Their query whether Athens had anything to do with Jerusalem proved to be exaggerated, certainly; yet it can serve to remind us forcibly of the care required in allowing a philosophical idiom to tailor one's theological inquiry.

The issue turns on a key point: how does one *resolve* a dispute? If one looks to philosophy as a criterion of judgment, we have the spectacle of entire portions of religious faith and practice being disallowed by one generation, often to be recovered by the next. (Hume's antipathy to miracles or more recent allergies to "myth" offer two useful examples.) If one employs the *habitus* of philosophy rather to elucidate a religious tradition more rigorously, one risks being thought less "critical" by one's contemporaries yet may well contribute more effectively to the continuing discussion. Everything turns here on the *use* to which a systematic ordering language is put.

I have argued that the major figures have never attempted to replace the God of Abraham with a philosophical substitute, but rather used their penchant for rigorous reflection to remove certain obstacles to belief in God which can easily and understandably arise (1975). Since fresh obstacles can arise with each cultural shift, the task is never completed, but a look back at the different forms it has taken offers an illustrative survey of methods in theology. There is a tradition of theological reflection as well as of religious life and practice, and one value of Lonergan's articulated view of method is his grasp and appreciation of that considerable fact. To note and to assess the shift in uses allows one to offer a more useful synthetic statement.

Lonergan eschews a unitary method in theology, wishing to accommodate the disciplines appropriate to the various religious studies, yet to transpose them from distinct fields to "functional specialties." The transposition is a critical one, and gives practical expression to his critical shift from theory to interiority. That is, "field specializations" will never become functional specialties until one has perceived how a particular field can subserve a larger shared inquiry, yet that perception does not represent a higher theory so much as a personal appropriation of the theological task—and the part one might play in continuing it. For the acquisition of more knowledge seldom allows one to see oneself as part of a larger enterprise; what is required is illumination of another order. Lonergan may weaken his own case by naming that gain "conversion," but the wary reader of *Method* will note how he spells out its various modes: intellectual, moral, and religious./4/ With this sophistication in mind, one can discern in his efforts an attempt to deal with a long-standing and vexing question: can one be a theologian and not believe, or must a theologian be a person of faith?

What should interest us more directly, however, is not the answer which Lonergan (or anyone else) might give to such a question, but *how* they set up their strategies for dealing with it. The critical move for Lonergan is the one noted: appreciating how one's *field* may become a functional specialty does not represent a theoretical advance, but already reflects a shift from theory to interiority. For what distinguishes fields are set procedures for inquiry which can yield coherent if not testable results. The advantages of such *collegia* are demonstrated in professional journals: colleagues can build on one another's results to effect a concerted inquiry. Recent advances in biblical studies are usually cited as a salient example.

Yet just as these gain momentum, certain especially astute voices will begin to question the sufficiency of the procedures. They will probably use the currency which Thomas Kuhn introduced into philosophy of science, questioning whether the received *paradigm* does not blind its devotés to dimensions of the subject matter which one can otherwise perceive to be worth pursuing. Scripture studies are no exception to this rule, as current disquietude displays (cf. Barr, Frei, Kelsey). Anyone arguing the need for a fresh approach cannot claim, of course, that their proposal will not itself be vulnerable to a similar critique. That is indeed beside the point, for they will be noting lacunae in an accepted approach by appealing to wider human concerns. It is not necessary to be in possession of an overarching theory to note inadequacies, though the logic of collaborative inquiry will demand that one formulate one's alternatives as systematically as possible.

With this clarification we can see that Lonergan's proposal that we learn how to *regard* the specialization proper to distinct fields as a functional specialty does not entail dismantling the theoretical mode of inquiry proper to one's field. Theory is indeed required to make corporate advances in learning possible. What he rather proposes is that we will participate in a theological effort precisely in the measure that we realize how such theoretical inquiry is part of something larger. And if that realization is not itself theoretical, it is no less precise for that. It amounts to gaining sufficient perspective on one's work that one can speak of "following a *paradigm*"—for that language already presupposes a reflective grasp of one's own inquiry.

Lonergan calls such a grasp *interior*. One might have preferred *critical*, yet would have to acknowledge how many a "critical study" falls short of being self-critical, which is just the note which Lonergan wants to strike. By insisting that such a reflective grasp is not *theoretical*, I have been alluding to the philosophical discussion of conceptual frameworks emanating from Carnap, as well as trying to parse Lonergan's own characterization of his efforts as formulating a shift from theory to interiority./5/ Furthermore, there is more at stake in theology than in philosophy of science, so the resistances to self-criticism will be that much more formidable. Besides customary myopia, institutional inertia, and conspiracies of funding—as if these were not enough!—theological inquiry probes close to our endemic self-deception as well. Sin is not only a topic in theology, but the quality of self-awareness required to use religious language properly will demand exposing dimensions of ourselves normally guarded from our own scrutiny (Hauerwas:89–95). The reasons for this will become clearer as we look more closely at that language itself. I mention them here only to clarify further the distinction Lonergan invokes between theory and interiority, and to suggest how his approach might prepare us better to assess the relationship between a theologian and his or her life of faith.

I have so far made use of Lonergan's approach in *Method in Theology* without much expounding it. I do so because I want to show my indebtedness without becoming entangled in exposition. Readers of *Method* will be able to test the adequacy of my treatment. I am not concerned to delineate the scope of the diverse functional specialties—research, interpretation, history, and dialectic; followed in turn by foundations, doctrine systematics, and communication—so much as to mark the shift involved in situating oneself and one's field *functionally*. I have identified that very shift with the move from theory to interiority which Lonergan associates with the dimension which critical reflection requires be added to classical modes of inquiry. I have suggested—albeit quite implicitly—that such a move already involves a kind of conversion, and so find the label of interiority a useful one. Again, readers of Lonergan may find it strange to locate conversion at the very point of adopting the overall scheme. But we should never forget that various modes of conversion obtain, and my goal is to show how this one is also involved in understanding the proper uses of religious language.

By linking the conversion from theory to interiority with analogy and narrative, I hope to show how one can make fruitful use of philosophical rigor in doing theology. I will also try to show how such an intellectual and spiritual deepening in fact grounds one's theological inquiry without thereby becoming a special theoretical field. The quest for foundations, in other words, is no less chimerical in theology than in philosophy—in fact, it is that much more so since a particular community must needs be the vehicle of a religious tradition (Hauerwas:15–39). Finally, expounders of Lonergan will have to square this approach with his singling out *foundations* as a functional specialty. We must be more concerned here with the grammar of the matter than with a particular expression.

Analogy and Narrative

The ordinary quest for foundations is a quite natural one. It expresses the intellectual demand that our conclusions offer sufficient warrant to justify one's accepting them. What could be misleading, however, is the way the metaphor of *foundations* can lead us to look for an indubitable starting point. In inveighing against the quest for foundations, I am taking my stand with philosophers like Charles Sanders Peirce and more recently Stephen Toulmin—to name but two—who have reminded us that arguments are warranted not so much by indubitable premises as by their structure. One must begin somewhere, indeed, and we can only hope for particularly perceptive people to suggest a fruitful starting point. The strategic *point de départ* of any specialized inquiry, Aristotle reminded us, is ever a matter of intuition (98a30). What can be monitored, however, is the care with which one draws conclusions; and it is these entailments, of course, which spell out the import of the starting point. An argument *shows* its formal validity, and its fruitfulness is displayed in its consequences. It is this characteristic which gives inquiry its public features, rather than the impossible demand that the premises be acceptable to all. For an argument is not grounded in its premises so much as it is warranted by the progress it is able to make in elucidating the point at issue.

These formal observations are of special import to theological inquiry. For the demand that one find a starting point common to believers and unbelievers alike will prevent one from recovering the specificity of a particular religious faith. It makes one try to assert what the Christian revelation *really* amounts to—say "pure unbounded love"—and blithely overlooks the ambiguities of such a notion to be coherent. The search for an undubitable starting point leads invariably to a formulation at once too vague to perform the task of elucidation and too ambiguous to function as a first premise.

Indeed theological inquiry shows the inadequacy of a foundational strategy more dramatically even than phenomenalism or other candidates from the history of philosophy. For religion as we have come to know it is a matter of historic communities bearing a revelation, expressing and developing it in worship and practice. Although each major religion presents itself as worthy of universal acceptance, *what* is preached and lived expresses a particular creed, code and cult. Yet its promises must be able to be understood, and here one requires some form of philosophical elucidation. My polemic against a foundational model should not be taken as a wholesale rejection of reason, but as a preliminary effort to retail an alternative approach.

I have mentioned Peirce, and incorporated Wittgenstein's reminders about arguments *showing* their warrants, to offer some guides to my philosophical orientation. My recipe for respecting both particular revelations and universal aspirations, however, rests on an analysis of the semantic structure of properly religious discourse. I shall maintain that the key expressions—no matter how common—remain systematically ambiguous, and that this (formal) fact dictates a specific strategy as a "theory of analogy," but rather in a series of reminders about the ways we can and do negotiate analogous expressions (Burrell, 1973). As I have suggested above, the adequacy of this argument will show itself in its capacity to illuminate one'a actual practice in using such language.

We must not then look for a theory, but are rather invited to look to our own usage and sharpen our consciousness of its actual conditions. Rather than demand criteria *tout court*, we are reminded that many such criteria are already operative in our reasoning, and asked to scrutinize the ways we *use* the ones we do rely upon. Here is where I find Lonergan's manifold use of 'conversion' to be useful, for the movements just proposed constitute a turn-about for most of us from a graduate seminar training that taught us how to ask for criteria. We are invited to pose the critical questions with more subtlety and self-awareness—greater interiority, if you will. Parallel to Wittgenstein's conversion from *Tractatus* to *Investigations*, we are counseled to ask not for the meaning but for the use.

That counsel itself, of course, can too quickly become yet another slogan. Its special relevance to theological argument comes from the fact that key religious expressions invariably demand elucidation because they must be used analogously. The reason is twofold: the expressions we have recourse to are themselves ambiguous—susceptible of many meanings; and this ambiguity must be systematically exploited to use them coherently of divinity or of the relations between creator and creation. That is, we must learn how the many meanings can be related to one, and how to display that relationship in our exposition. Only by using ambiguous expressions in an ordered fashion can their ambiguity become systematic enough to call them analogous terms. The difference between ambiguous and analogous expressions lies in using them systematically—that is, so as to *show* how the many uses can be related to one./6/

We accomplish this, quite simply, by giving an example. Yet since examples are not ordinarily produced—as in kindergarten show-and-tell—but narrated, what we in fact do when we give an instance is tell a story. So, for example(!), we can illustrate the shifts in accent during a lifetime of a couple's avowing "I love you" by sketching the different circumstances attending their twenty-fifth anniversary from their second. And in doing so, we can do justice to two concomitant assertions: that they meant what they said to each other on their second anniversary, and yet from the vantage point of their twenty-fifth, they will wonder whether they even knew what they were saying twenty-three years before. What has shifted, of course, is their point of reference: the paradigm instances which offer the primary analogate for their ordered use of the term. Their earlier avowal seems so remote from their current paradigm—what they have discovered loving one another to be and to entail—that it seems barely to qualify for inclusion in the notion. Yet a more extended narrative—a life story—should be able to trace those shifts in a sufficiently ordered way to indicate the connections, however dramatic the shifts may have been./7/

This story of how we tell stories to elucidate our current paradigm for ordering ambiguous notions has a single point. It intends to remind us that we can use such expressions responsibly even though we may be unable to formulate an unambiguous definition, say, of love. Put otherwise: analogous expressions do not require a univocal "core of meaning" to tether them to responsible use. Much as we might *think* they should, we can and do use them otherwise. And if we attend to our use (rather than to a theory of meaning), we will note that what shifts is the paradigmatic use to and by which we order the others: the primary analogate. And the story of those shifts—tantamount to a life-story—offers sufficient coherence to assure us we are using the same notion. If no such story can be forged, of course, we have sheer ambiguity—just as a variety of viewpoints may never become pluralistic but remain simply diverse.

So a systematically ambiguous expression will be distinguished from a merely ambiguous one by our ability to link the successive paradigmatic uses by a coherent or unifying story. How does one determine whether a story is coherent or not? There is no litmus test for coherence, of course, yet literary critics manage to discriminate among stories even though their judgments remain contestable. There is no alternative, however, for the nature of the expressions we use defies univocal rendering. Any attempt so to define *loving* will itself involve ambiguous terms, and these will require to be elucidated in turn by salient examples. This semantic fact clinches the case: it is not simply that we may be unable to find an unambiguous formula for *loving*, but that it is impossible to find one. So recourse to narrative illustration is not a *faute de mieux*; there simply is no better way.

The more positive side of the story reminds us that we are driven to use essentially contestable notions to express what transcends our experience, yet translates our aspirations. Here we have the reason why religious language must needs employ ambiguous expressions, and why the theological task becomes one of relating the many uses to one in such a way as to display the transcendent character of the notion. Over against an insistence that loving cannot be gainful to both (and in that sense reciprocal), one can offer a trajectory of selflessness—of disinterested or detached regard for the other—where we can recognize gradations in the purity of one's love. Taking such a projection to the limit will in fact be unimaginable for us, but not incoherent, for one can recognize an implicit gradient in selflessness (Burrell, 1979a:87–89).

Classical authors have called attention to the difference by contrasting *satisfaction* with *delight*. The capacity for expressing the transcendent is linked to the potential for self-transcendence in individuals. So the analogous use of inherently ambiguous terms to express transcendence is linked to just such a self-realization—what Lonergan called *interiority*. In the measure that we can be aware of using an expression beyond its normal reach, because we have come to experience that term's ability to render our own aspirations at various points of attainment or failure, then we can be said to be using it *properly*. It is of such awareness that analogous usage is born, and in developing that awareness it is warranted. Here is where grammar dictates certain practices, practices more traditionally associated with monasteries than with academe. It is, to speak more abstractly, where theology and spirituality intersect.

Lest that bold statement allow some to write off my proposal as irrational, or accuse me of resolving in "mysticism," allow me to review the inner link between the need to employ such expressions to elucidate a religious tradition, and the demand that we tether our elucidations by narrating instances. What such a pointed use of narrative allows one to do is to test whether the paradigmatic use of the expositor is anywhere near my own— for we quite naturally relate ourselves to a narrative account. Even if our stories are relatively distant one from another, that distance can nonetheless be factored in. And more often than not, an unaccustomed example may solicit dimensions in me which I have left fallow but which call me to a fuller sense of myself. For that is how narratives work: reading another's triggers my own.

So we are called not merely to adjudicate the coherence of another's story, but to see whether the account it solicits from ourselves is adequate to what we aspire to in common. If the other's story triggers no aspiration at all in me, then nothing is shared and we have no communication. It is as though sheer ambiguity reigns. Cultural differences can certainly be great enough to have such an effect. But the other can happen as well. There are no external criteria here—the point of the use of narrative in theological argument is to lead us to recognize the relevant relationships we bear to one another, and so judge for ourselves how much we aspire in common.

A Critical Moment and Task

I have argued so far to the necessity for narrative accounts as an integral part of theological argumentation. The pervasive presence of analogous terms demands that we locate the prime analogates if our premises are to have the consistency they need to allow consequences to be drawn. (This has been a constant concern since Aristotle: once we recognize the presence of a class of expressions neither univocal nor simply ambiguous, how can we control their use sufficiently so that argumentation can proceed?) By elaborating the context with salient examples, we can establish the sense of the term which is paradigmatic for this argument. And providing salient examples means telling opposite tales.

What is more, it is the failure to supply instances which leads to confusion here. An ideal of systematization which overlooks the need to identify the primary senses of the terms in question in effect presumes the key terms to be univocal. For that is what is demanded by pure (or abstract) argument. Yet by overlooking the fact that theological terms are structurally ambiguous, we lose the opportunity to fix that ambiguity systematically. As a result, what appears to be rigorous argument in fact confuses the issues and fails to advance the inquiry. Theology offers abundant evidence supporting Wittgenstein's warning philosophers away from fixed conceptions of rigor, and returning us to the Aristotelian observation that there is a rigor appropriate to each discipline.

In effect, then, a theological argument scheme may be quite simple in structure, yet demand considerable narrative amplification. We can speak, certainly, of examples illustrating, so long as we realize that such illustration is far more than decoration: without it the terms cannot function as analogous terms must in argument./8/ So it would trivialize my meta-argument to caricature it as advice to theologians to begin telling stories. The stories are part of the argument; scheme and narrative reinforce one another. The advice rather is to let oneself be liberated from a procrustean ideal of rigor, and to note the considerable clarification realized by stories aptly selected and told, and the necessity for employing them. I have also directed our attention to an ironic result of letting ourselves be guided by an inappropriate ideal: it is such argument which founders on the ambiguities latent in the key expressions left to float free. In more colloquial speech, we can explain our impression about so much theological writing: how quickly it becomes gas!

So storytelling, however necessary to theological argument, will never suffice. It must be at the service of a goal, and part of a larger reasoned discourse which can be communicated systematically. Doctrinal formulations are of this sort, of course, and my emphasis on the role narrative plays in clarifying the key terms employed shows why Lonergan places the functional specialty of *doctrine* after the effort to establish a foundational framework, which itself follows upon the entire process of research, interpretation, history and the interplay of dialectics. Once we realize all that went into a doctrinal statement, we will be less sanguine about their capacity to carry a tradition. They function as a useful shorthand, or a set of grammatical rules, neither of which can be utilized without the living context of language use—in this case, of worship and practice. So the continuing community insures the proper use of doctrine as much or more than doctrine safeguards a community. Or to exploit the customary metaphor of *safeguarding*: a security force is as effective as the social bonding at work in a society.

It is this interplay between rules of grammar and the demands upon a language in use that constitute the living criteria which help us settle for an appropriate framework. When religious expressions are demanded to make sense of our situation, we must press the received rules for their use into action. This test amounts to a critical reappropriation of a tradition, and always includes an element of revision. By noting the role which narration of key experiences will play in this process, and by articulating the process in linguistic terms, I hope to have illustrated what is going on better that the more customary (and more abstract) discussion of a "dialectic between theory and practice" (or even worse, *praxis*). Yet for those wedded to such language, this is what I am referring to, although it should be clear by now how the use of story can help bridge what looks to be—and often is—so intractable a gap as that between *theory* and *practice*.

For what stories do is to remind us that the critical assessments demanded of any argument cannot, in the theological argument, escape criticizing our own participation in the practices which are ingredient to understanding religious language. We cannot hope, in this domain, to be critical without becoming self-critical. For the clarification demanded and promised by critical intelligence can only derive from that crucible wherein we must press religious expressions into service to make sense of our human situation. Yet we can only explore their adequacy to the task by becoming that much clearer about them ourselves. And such a process of clarification inevitably asks us to take their implications more surely to heart, and test them in our practice. Indeed one can fairly say that if this does not happen we can quite surely judge ourselves to have been dealing with a religious ideology rather than a religious faith. Crises of faith are of this sort, and if one cannot learn how to use the received language effectively, or extend it appositely, then that person must look elsewhere for continued guidance.

Perhaps I have said enough to illustrate how the semantic structure of religious language affects theological argument, and to offer a fruitful commentary on the shift which Lonergan identifies as from theory to interiority. My own argument has been structured with stories in mind and often alluded to. I have chosen this mode to make us aware of how it is that we function when we reason. As a meta-argument, the stories regard our use of theological models rather than the issues those models have sought to illuminate. If this gave my presentation a somewhat abstracted air, that must be seen as a consequence of dealing at second remove, as it were. For I have had in each case an approach in mind, hoping that my readers would identify it sufficiently to prompt reflection (cf. Burrell, 1979b).

If analogous expressions can only be used responsibly when accompanied by the requisite commentary of an apposite story, such stories will fail to do their work if we persist in thinking of them as *mere* illustrations. Yet not even a doctrinaire Hegelian can fail to be caught off guard by a pointed rabbinic tale. So one can hope, at best, that if theologians grasp the significance of this exposition, that they will begin to let us know—by a narrative of sorts—where they stand as they employ the terms they do. And should that begin, theologians might even be moved enough by the illustrations they will need to give, to become self-critical in turn. Then we would be at least moving towards that deeper unity which could link the diverse specialties of religious studies: an interiority expressed in worship and in practice.

The personal task of appropriating criteria to the point of self-criticism entails a social (or institutional) one as well. For the proliferation of academic specializations has the concomitant effect of minimizing my need to take a stand on any substantive point. For fields are so arranged that doing so requires one to cross disciplines, and so be rendered doubly vulnerable. Yet it was to prepare ourselves to make substantive judgments that we early committed ourselves to a liberal education! Ironies abound in academe as elsewhere, of course, nor should it surprise a student of history or human nature that institutional arrangements firmly embody our favorite avoidance syndromes. Nine years of experience as department chair have taught me how formidable a task it is to work against this organizational inertia. Yet it cannot be overlooked, for the appropriation of criteria demands a favorable climate. Without the continuing conceptual and organizational efforts of a faculty to find the appropriate institutional expression, schemes like Lonergan's (or Pannenberg's) for ordering inquiry in theology are in danger of remaining idle recommendations. We should not need Marx to have reminded us how the structures governing our daily interaction affect our intellectual perspective. Clarification calls forth correlative creative efforts— in ourselves and in shaping our respective environments.

NOTES

/1/   Kierkegaard displayed consummate skill in using pseudonyms to elicit the self-critical awareness requisite to theological reflection, yet it took philosophers more than a century to appreciate the import of this skill. I am indebted to Bernard Lonergan (1957) for the fundamental key to self-appropriation of modes of argument. Cf. Burrell, 1972, and Crowe, 59–62.

/2/   The story of Adam and Eve presents an archetypal avoidance pattern; Fingarette's analysis of self-deception suggests a useful philosophical strategy for elucidating so pervasive a human practice.

/3/   Schubert Ogden makes his case for "process theology" in terms of an "adequate conceptualization." The case I am making for the necessity of analogous discourse renders that criterion unstable.

/4/   Lonergan's use of 'conversion' needs to be traced first to the "intellectual conversion" proper to (1957), and even may be anticipated in his rendering of Aquinas's *conversio ad phantasmata* (1967). Clearly 'conversion' is an ambiguous term.

/5/   There is considerable current philosophical discussion on "conceptual frameworks." The point I wish to make stems more directly from Carnap's observation that the "choice" of a framework is not itself a conceptual issue—lest one initiate a regress. Lonergan's chapter on "Things" (1957) offers a useful introduction to the question.

/6/   I am here resuming the argument of (1973).

/7/   Hence one's inclination to keep citing Augustine's *Confessions* as a paradigm of storied self-awareness. Cf. my interpretative chapter (1975).

/8/   Paul Holmer develops this point by noting how *philosophical* is Kierkegaard's use of examples, in McInerny.

WORKS CONSULTED

Augustine, Aurelius
1961   *Confessions.* Trans. R. S. Pine-Coffin. Baltimore: Penguin.

Barr, James
1973   *Bible in Modern World.* New York: Harper & Row.

Burrell, David
1972   "Method and Sensibility: Novak's Debt to Lonergan." *Journal of the American Academy of Religion* 40:349–67.
1975   *Analogy and Philosophical Language.* New Haven: Yale University Press.
1973   *Exercises in Religious Understanding.* Notre Dame: University of Notre Dame Press.
1979a   *Aquinas: God and Action.* Notre Dame: University of Notre Dame Press.
1979b   "Theology and the linguistic turn." *Communio* 6:95–112.

Carnap, Rudolph
1956   *Meaning and Necessity.* 2nd ed. Chicago: University of Chicago Press.

Crowe, Frederick
1980   *Lonergan Enterprise.* Boston: Cowley.

Fackenheim, Emil
1970   *Religious Dimension in Hegel's Thought.* Boston: Beacon.

Fingarette, Herbert
1969   *Self-Deception.* New York: Humanities.

Frei, Hans
1974   *Eclipse of Biblical Narrative.* New Haven: Yale University Press.

Hauerwas, Stanley
1977   *Truthfulness and Tragedy*. Notre Dame: University of Notre Dame Press.

Kelsey, David
1975   *Uses of Scripture in Recent Theology*. Philadelphia: Fortress.

Kuhn, Thomas
1970   *Structure of Scientific Revolutions*. Chicago: University of Chicago Press.

Lonergan, Bernard
1957   *Insight: A Study of Human Understanding*. London: Longmans.
1967   *Verbum: Word and Idea in Aquinas*. Notre Dame: University of Notre Dame Press.
1972   *Method in Theology*. London: Darton, Longman and Todd.

McInerny, Ralph
1968   *New Themes in Christian Philosophy*. Nortre Dame: University of Notre Dame Press.

Ogden, Schubert
1966   *Reality of God*. New York: Harper & Row.

Pannenberg, Wolfhart
1976   *Theology and the Philosophy of Science*. Philadelphia: Westminster.

Peirce, Charles Sanders
1973   *Essential Writings*. Ed. Edward Moore. New York: Harper & Row.

Toulmin, Stephen
1964   *Uses of Argument*. Cambridge: Cambridge University Press.

Wittgenstein, Ludwig
1953   *Philosophical Investigations*. New York: Macmillan.
1974   *Tractatus Logico-Philosophicus*. New York: Humanities.

Morality, Judgment, and Prayer

Robert O. Johann

My purpose in this essay is to develop a conception of reason as primarily practical and to suggest its relevance to a philosophy of religion. When reason is viewed as purely cognitive and separate from appetite, the rational subject is deprived of any standard for appraising alternative options that is intrinsic to himself as rational. All his standards must be derived from his extrarational interests. This is the basis for the usual lament that in matters of value there is ultimately no neutral or archimedean point from which to decide between conflicting judgments. Such judgments are all ultimately relative to individual wants or at best to the particular cultures and forms of life in which the standards they are based on have been developed, and the process of deliberation which they conclude, lacking any pretension to universal validity, is inevitably rejected as a genuine way to knowledge.

This, however, is changed when reason itself is seen as an interest structure or appetite. For then it finds within itself, as part of its own nature and not as something borrowed, the norm and basis of choice. As the interest underlying and intrinsic to all rational activity and all questioning, it is itself beyond question, the norm of norms, the final standard. It does not indeed constrain inquiry from the outside—there are, I agree, no such constraints. Neither does it preclude argument or automatically settle disputes. It provides rather a base on which disputes may proceed rationally. For its function is to illumine inquiry from within, serving as the question to which inquiry seeks the answer and in the light of which the inquirer can appraise competing, would-be solutions.

Such is my overall theme. I want to assert the primacy of practical judgment over the purely theoretical, not only to find a place for deliberation about the good as a genuine way to knowledge but to show how it is central to all inquiry, and to see, finally, what this might mean in the domain of religion. As I proceed, it will be evident how heavily I rely on the insights of John Dewey but also, especially in the last part of the paper, where I depart from what he would accept.

The paper falls into three parts. First I argue the case for deliberation as a way to genuine knowledge in the realm of morality. If the case cannot be made there, it cannot be made anywhere. I then explore the ultimately deliberative character of all inquiry. Finally, I sketch briefly what I take to be some of the import of this conception for a philosophy of religion.

1.

Perhaps the best way to begin our investigation is to take up the question raised by Richard Rorty at the end of his Presidential Address to the APA. After sympathetically portraying pragmatism as aiming to deconstruct the traditional "notions of truth as correspondence, of knowledge as discovery of essense, of morality as obedience to principle" (735) and after arguing that for the pragmatist "there are no constraints on inquiry save conversational ones—no wholesale constraints derived from the nature of objects, or of the mind, or of language, but only those retail constraints provided by the remarks of our fellow-inquirers" (726), Rorty raises, without trying to settle it, the issue about irrationalism. The central question about this whole approach is "whether we can be pragmatists without betraying Socrates, without falling into irrationalism" (731). If there is no permanent and atemporal reality over against the thinker that can serve as the measure of his thought, something to which thought can conform and so be true or, to put it another way, if "our culture, or purposes, or intuitions cannot be supported except conversationally" (728), how argue successfully with the would-be despot who wants no part of the conversation but simply to have his own way? If there is nothing "permanent and unhistorical which explains *why* we should continue to converse" (733) nor anything which might guarantee convergence to agreement, then what defense can we muster against our own less noble instincts when we ourselves are tempted to withdraw from the conversation to go in unbridled pursuit of our individual desires?

That the only alternatives confronting the philosopher are either to hold onto some basic foundational constraint or resign himself to intellectual and moral chaos, believing "that either there are rock bottom permanent standards of objectivity and rationality or there is only 'mere' rhetoric" (Bernstein:771), would seem to be a position not uncommon among moral theorists. Thus, the lack of constraining moral facts at the basis of moral theory, facts which are what they are independently of anyone's personal stance, leads Joseph Margolis to maintain that "men are, and cannot help being, moral partisans" (5), and that the business of the moral philosopher is concerned with conceptually clarifying competing theories but, except for "exposing some conceptual weakness . . . of given alternatives" (6) in no way deciding between them. Again, Alan Donagan rejects as philosophically fraudulent the position on moral deliberation of what he calls the new intuitionists precisely because it lacks "a procedure for ascertaining the weight of each consideration, either comparatively or absolutely, a procedure analogous to that of putting objects on a balance or scale" (23).

This leaves everyone with the task of having, in the final analysis, to make up his own mind, judge for himself, in moral matters. Since the theory does not predetermine the conclusion to be reached, the individual moral agent is on his own and "ordinarily respectable persons [are allowed] to do anything they are likely to choose, and to have a good conscience in doing it" (23)—a laxist position, Donagan feels, if ever there was one. And as a final example of this flight from judgment, consider the position of John Rawls on the nature of moral theory. As he sees it, moral philosophy does not aim to understand or make sense of the process of moral deliberation but rather to undergird or ground its end products. The idea is to construct a theoretical framework from which specific judgments matching our considered convictions might be derived by strictly logical procedures (46). In other words, moral theory looks to transforming a problem of moral choice into one of rational choice, where rationality is understood technologically, i.e., as "taking effective means to achieve one's ends" (401). Instead of illuminating the deliberative process, it seeks to eliminate it, or at least find a more reliable substitute for it, one that can guarantee agreement.

In each of these cases, the process of making up one's mind about what ends to pursue, what commitments to make, is felt to be too chancy and subjective to claim rational respect. If a procedure is rational in the measure that it can generate unconstrained consensus,/1/ then moral deliberation, the process of determining categorical norms, hardly seems to qualify. Interestingly enough, even Rorty, after seemingly subscribing to the pragmatic view that the pattern of all inquiry is deliberation, fails to take the process of genuine deliberation seriously as an alternative to foundationalism. For, whereas to deliberate is to raise questions about what norms *deserve* our allegiance, Rorty seems to think that the rejection of ultimate foundations makes such questioning impossible and leaves one with no alternative but to follow the accepted standards of one's society. Indeed, I would suggest that it is precisely because Rorty sees pragmatism only negatively as a program of deconstruction, precisely because he fails to explore the idea of rationality as basically deliberative that an acceptance of the pragmatic standpoint appears to him to leave us with no defense against irrationality. A main point of what follows is to make up for that failure.

2.

Rorty is correct in connecting a deliberative concept of rationality with a rejection of truth as pictorial (722). Deliberation is not a matter of discovering what is the case, of bringing the mind into conformity with what already exists. It is concerned rather with what should be brought about, with determining an appropriate rule of action. As Dewey would put it, deliberation is forward looking, not backward looking; its focus is consequent, not antecedent, reality. But, while to say this is to reject a pictorial notion of truth, it is not necessarily to reject any and every correspondence theory of truth. As a matter of fact, Dewey is quite explicit in developing such a theory./2/ His whole point however, is to suggest another way for the mind to correspond to reality than simply to re-present what is already there. And it is here that Dewey proposes the image not of a picture corresponding to its subject matter, but of a key corresponding to a lock (1946:343). In other words, the relationship is not static but dynamic. Dewey writes: "What makes any proposition scientific [and, in the context, scientific is equivalent to warranted and true] is its power to yield understanding, insight, intellectual at-homeness, in connection with any existential state of affairs" (1958:163). The truth of a proposition thus becomes its functional correspondence to an otherwise problematic situation. It is grasped as true when it is grasped in this functional role of settling or making sense of a situation that would otherwise remain indeterminate and unsettled. From this point of view, inquiry as deliberation and truth as correspondence, far from being incompatible, actually require one another. For only insofar as the various proposals being deliberatively considered *correspond* to a greater or lesser extent to the practical requirements of the situation provoking the inquiry is the inquiring mind in any position to prefer one to another. In this light, supporting a proposal with reasons is not a matter of showing how the mind is "in touch with physical reality, or the moral law, or the real numbers, or some other sort of object patiently waiting about to be copied" (Rorty:728). It is rather a matter of pointing to those features of it which render it more likely to resolve the problem being addressed than any of the alternatives to which it is being compared.

What is primary, then, in determining the appropriateness of a proposal is the question which is being asked and which the proposal is supposed to answer. It is the question and the intention of sense that animates it which measure the relevance of whatever is proposed as an answer. But the question here is not something abstract and extrinsic to the inquiry. It is the concrete reality of the searching, inquiring self. To be engaged in inquiry is to exist as an interest in sense, a quest for sense. What triggers inquiry is, on the one hand, the agent's need to act (where action is understood as responding to a situation in the light of an interpretive judgment of what it makes sense to do) and, on the other, the indeterminateness for the agent of just what action is called for. In other words, the situation presents itself as indeterminate in its practical significance and in need of judicial settlement. Inquiry is the practical undertaking on the part of the agent to supply what is needed—it is his effort to reconstruct the sense of the situation and so interpret its meaning that precisely as an agent, he is no longer at a loss but rather is newly at home. The validity (or truth) of a judgment is its capacity to do this, to meet the needs of the situation, to satisfy the conditions of the problem—a problem, be it noted, that is ultimately rooted in the very being of the rational agent. For, to be called on to act is to be a practical intention of sense and concrete reasonableness; it is to be a being whose activity and its results require his own approval but who can approve of his life and his world only insofar as they are had as adding up, only insofar as they are experienced as making sense.

The words "had" and "experienced" in the preceding sentence are being used as Dewey means them. The problematic character of the situation which provokes inquiry and the sense which terminates it are both immediately qualitative states of affairs which in Dewey's terminology are had, not known. Knowledge on the other hand is a matter of the warranted assertibility of propositions (not a grasp of essence, be it remarked), and propositions enjoy this trait to the extent that, as implicit directives, they organize and settle the sense of a situation. Hence Dewey's famous definition of inquiry. It is, he writes, "the controlled or directed transformation of an indeterminate situation into one that is so determinate in its constituent distinctions and relations as to convert the elements of the original situation into a unified whole" (1938:104). The emphasis on "wholeness" here, which is not uncommon in his descriptions of the consummatory in experience, highlights the fundamentally aesthetic character of intelligence for Dewey. But it should not be thought that the inquiring mind has to start from scratch and construct a "whole" from a collection of unrelated items. The situation is not originally, nor can it be, wholly indeterminate. Were it so, panic, and not rational inquiry, would seem the only course open. Rather, it is indeterminate in some or other respect that requires practical attention./3/ Hence, the transformation involved in inquiry consists in the determination of that course of action which fits into and meshes with the larger and unquestioned scheme of the agent's life. It is a matter of settling a particular issue, of retail, not wholesale, resolutions.

In this connection one is reminded of H. Richard Niebuhr's image of man as "responsible self." The idea or pattern of responsibility, he writes, is the "idea of an agent's action as response to an action upon him in accordance with his interpretation of the latter action [and this interpretation, Niebuhr points out, will be part of a more comprehensive and 'relatively consistent scheme of interpretations'] and with his expectation of a response to his response; and all of this is in a continuing community of agents" (65). The image is of man as participant in an ongoing dialogue which is a continuous joint creation, but where the contributions, if they are to be such, are under the constraint of fitting in with what has gone before and of moving it forward. Inquiry, in Dewey's sense, occurs when it is not clear what would constitute an appropriate contribution. The artist steps back from the canvas in an effort to determine that touch, that stroke which will enhance, and not nullify, what is already there. It will be what it ought to be, not when it conforms to some antecedent prescription, but when it fits, when it corresponds.

At this point, however, a distinction is called for—a distinction some-what blurred by Niebuhr's image. For our actions can be conceived as "fitting into" two quite different contexts. The distinction between the contexts corresponds to the classic distinction between "making" and "doing" which in turn stems from the different ways one can view human activity. One way is to look at action from the outside, as it were—i.e., not precisely as something intended, but simply in terms of the empirical change(s) it brings about. This is action as "making," as effecting a new empirical situation. From this point of view, an action is had as making sense in proportion as it transforms the world in accordance with the agent's desires. It is thus the empirical interests of the agent which structure the context into which his actions (as makings) are intended to fit. Were he uninterested in the determinate outcome of his actions, he would have no basis for preferring one to another. On the other hand, to the extent an action changes the world in accordance with the agent's desires, i.e., to the extent that it empirically satisfies, there is no question but that to such an extent it makes sense. The inherent aim of action as making, therefore, is to satisfy the agent's empirical interests. And since what will do this is a matter of empirical fact, its determination by the agent must proceed along empirical lines, i.e., by trial and error, observation and experiment. In other words, action as making will make sense not because the agent wants it to or intends that it should but solely to the extent that the changes it actually effects are correlative to his empirical wants.

Action as "doing," on the other hand, is action viewed from the inside. That is to say, it is action precisely as meant, as issuing from an intentional source. If action as making is the determination of the empirical world and of its relation to the agent as himself an empirical interest-structure, action as doing is a determination of the agent as agent, i.e., not as something given and determinate but as himself a determiner. It is a specific actualization of his very capacity to act, to take an intentional stand, a matter of self-position and self-definition. As such, it presupposes a context in which meaning and intent make a difference, a context in which an action has import not only in terms of its effects, but also by reason of its source, precisely as something willed.

Now, the only context which meets these requirements is the interper-sonal one. It is the context of persons in mutual relation with one another, the context provided by on-going communication. From this point of view, an action will be had as fitting in or making sense in the measure it is consistent with this mutuality of the personal. The intention informing it must harmonize with intending the other as partner and cosource of a common world, with intending the other as you. For, it should be noted, unlike the context structured by the agent's empirical interests, the context of persons in mutual relation, the communicative context, is never mere matter of fact, but always matter of intention. Persons can exist in mutual relation only if they intend to. In like manner, an action, as intended, fits into this context, only if it is regulated by this constitutive intention. Thus, whereas action as change can make sense accidentally, i.e., if it happens to transform the world in a manner conforming to what the agent's interests happen to be, action as doing can make sense only if it is meant to. Since, however, to regulate one's activity by the intention to maintain the mutuality of the personal is, it might be widely agreed, what it means to act morally,/4/ then it follows that one cannot act morally by accident. Also, whereas actions as transformations make sense if they satisfy the agent's interests, actions as doings make sense only if they are moral. To be immoral, on the other hand, is to reject the effort to make sense of one's doings. It is to posit oneself and determine the world without regard for the personal other whose presence one's own doings presuppose.

It follows from this that a moral quality is inherent in every action. Just as every action determines the world in a way that is consistent or not with the agent's own interests, so also, since that world is essentially a shared world, and present to the agent as shared, he cannot act without either expressly taking that awareness into account and acting accordingly or expressly disregarding it. In other words, an agent cannot do anything intentionally without defining himself in the process as considerate and mindful of the personal other or as inconsiderate and unconcerned. His every act is ultimately either an acceptance of the interrelation of persons as normative for what he does or its rejection. It will be in answer to a quest for justice on his part, or a conscious evasion of the question.

Now the process of inquiry that seeks to determine what action in the situation is consistent with intending the other as you, or to put it another way, what action is consistent with intending the autonomy and equality of agents in relation to one another and the world they share, is moral deliberation. It is deliberation because it is the appraisal of various alternatives in the light of a practical aim. The aim provides the norm in the sense of defining the question which the practical judgment must answer. And one can appropriately term it moral deliberation because the normative aim is ultimate and universal. It is not a matter of the agent's asking what change in the situation will bring it into line with his own desires. He is seeking, rather, to determine himself in a way consistent with the intention any agent must have if his action as doing is to be rationally defensible, fit into the common world it presupposes, make sense. In short he is involved in the continuous and universal task of creating community, of coming to mutually acceptable terms with the other as *you*, of determining what is just.

From this point of view, the oversights of the moralists cited earlier become manifest. Moral considerations will not be simply "overriding considerations bearing on the conduct of one's own life and the lives of others as such" (8) no matter what those considerations happen to be, as

Margolis maintains. A moral consideration will be one that is relevant to the resolution of the moral question. And although anyone asking the moral question is always the product of a particular culture and history so that what presents itself as an answer to him cannot be unaffected by historical and cultural conditions, still the question itself (as well as the way to answer it) "is not regulated by actual groups but confronts possible groups to be created" (Kecskemeti:337). It is in this sense a kind of timeless task. Anyone asking it knows he is asking a question that transcends cultural diversity since the different cultures themselves and the norms they embody are all attempts to answer it. That is why Margolis' conception of the moral philosopher as basically a logician is really inadequate. Different purportedly moral judgments are not simply statements of different arbitrary over-riding preferences. If they are moral judgments at all, they are meant as answers to the moral question. They are tentative determinations of the rules to be followed for the mutual shaping of our common world and can be appraised accordingly. Those judgments or determinations are to be preferred, are simply better, which *precisely in relation to the question* being asked give rise to fewer, less serious, objections. Otherwise stated, the justification of a judgment is its capacity to settle a question, to put an end to a particular inquiry, to claim the assent of those who would otherwise remain puzzled or at odds about the issue it is supposed to resolve. This last is important. Apparent disagreement is intellectually significant only when the parties to it are really asking the same question, which most often is not the case. The fact that they are will not, of course, assure their coming to terms. But it will at least keep the inquirers from working at cross purposes. Moreover, for two or more parties to be jointly aiming at unconstrained agreement regarding the regulative meanings of their common life is already for them to be behaving morally toward one another. This, I suggest, is something we all know. Raising the moral question is the first step towards answering it, whereas refusing to raise it is already to be in the wrong, which means, of course, that however intractable some moral issues may be, not all are that way. And there are none on which it is impossible to make a start.

   These same ideas point up the problem of Rawls's position. He is trying to answer the moral question without asking it, and it simply cannot be done. Why he wants to do so is clear enough. He thinks, as we have indicated, that it is the function of moral theory to generate certain specific conclusions, *viz.*, our considered convictions about what it is right to do, rather than to evaluate the appropriateness of their being our convictions. That is why he tries to transform the moral question into a technical question. A technical question is about how to achieve a specific state of affairs (a specific end) and its answer is not only independent of what anyone intends but is publicly confirmable. A moral question, on the other hand, presupposes the moral intention, the intention of unconstrained consensus regarding the regulative meanings of our common life, and its answer requires deliberation and judgment. That is why we said earlier that it is impossible to act morally by accident. But the real root of Rawls's problem is his theoretical conception of reason. Unless reason is itself an interest structure, an unrestricted interest in sense, in the concrete reasonableness not only of our makings but of our doings, the moral question cannot even be asked. One can contrive a procedure to generate our considered convictions, but one cannot begin to explain why they deserve to be such. And that, I submit, is what moral deliberation and moral theory are all about.

That such deliberation, finally, is not philosophically fraudulent or morally laxist should also now be clear. Donagan, it will be recalled, objected that unless the precise weight to be given each competing consideration were settled beforehand, people would be left to make up their own minds on moral issues and could wind up doing anything they pleased with *a good conscience*. He thinks that making up one's own mind is indistinguishable from arbitrary choice. We have seen that this is not the case. Deliberation does move from the indeterminate to the determinate, from the unsettled to the settled. But so, we suggest, does all real inquiry. Really to ask a question is really to be undecided and open to different answers. It is also, however, to be aware of what might count as an answer, which is not just anything at all. Moreover, a specific answer can claim one's assent not by personal *fiat*, or because the one forming it *somehow* finds it satisfying, but only because it is actually experienced (*had*) as answering, settling, putting to rest, the issue which gave rise to it. In other words, to be deliberating is not to be bereft of norms. It is to let the question serve as norm. And what better claim to acceptance can our judgments have than that they actually answer our questions? Indeed, what I am arguing in this paper is that ultimately they have *no other* claim.

3.

I have dwelt so far on moral deliberation as a conspicuous example of a type of inquiry that is neither foundational nor irrational, that is both creative and nonarbitrary. Moral judgments remain, to be sure, inherently controversial. Each is as good or bad as the case that can be made for it (itself a matter of evaluative judgment), and there is nothing exterior to the process itself of inquiry and judgment by which its results may be tested or confirmed. As Bernstein has put it: "There is no way of escaping from human freedom and responsibility in making moral decisions, and no ultimate support to which we can appeal in making such decisions" (762). For all that, however, the results of moral deliberation do present themselves on occasion as having a claim upon our allegiance. If they are not susceptible to experimental testing in the manner of scientific constructs, neither are they had as pure and wholly unverifiable fictions (Kliever:168). That they should be thought such is simply the final working-out of the initial illusion that man is primarily a knower and that knowing is prior to doing. Rather, their validity consists, as we have seen, in their correspondence as answers to existential questions, in their capacity to settle satisfactorily a problematic and indeterminate existential state of affairs. Indeed, the problem addressed by moral judgments is the inclusive one of continually creating community. That is why, although no moral judgment (or principle) will necessarily command universal assent since a resolution to the moral question is neither necessarily nor universally intended, still we cannot make a moral judgment without believing, *pace* Bernstein (762), that it *ought* to command universal assent. A judgment which, in the eyes of the one who makes it satisfactorily resolves a problem which everyone faces and everyone ought to address, is *eo ipso* a judgment presenting itself as one that everyone ought to accept.

As I indicated from the beginning, however, my concern with the nature of moral inquiry is to illumine the nature of all inquiry. In other words, a main point in what I am saying is that it is not only the moral philosophers who have tried to escape having to make up their minds and sought instead to show how in some way "objective reality" had already made them up for them (or, since the latter was clearly not the case, that moral judgments are hopelessly subjective). Philosophers generally have followed the same route, and pretty much for the same reason. They are all aware that their judgments are not true simply because it is they who make them. If a person judges that such and such is the case, there has to be some basis for what he says, some reason for his assertion, if the latter is not to be arbitrary. But what satisfactory basis can there be other than the fact that that is how things are? Only their being this way is a relevant reason for claiming them to be so. Thus what is antecedently the case is the measure to which our judgments must conform to have a claim on our allegiance, and inquiry is simply the process of bringing our minds into correspondence with it. Or so, at least, it has seemed. The present crisis in the orders of meaning and value is simply the result of the growing realization that in these realms such correspondence is out of the question.

Here, however, is where the real significance of Dewey's reinterpretation of truth as correspondence comes in. He is not primarily interested in providing an answer to the above mentioned crisis, but aims to dissipate its presumed rationale. For, in his view, not only in the realm of practical truth is the correspondence of our judgments to antecedent reality impossible to ascertain. It is just as impossible in the realm of *theoria*. How, Dewey asks, can reality serve to measure the truth of our judgments if we only come to know that reality in and through our judgments?

> Such a view, like any strictly epistemological view, seems to me to assume a mysterious and unverifiable doctrine of pre-established harmony. How an event can be (i) what-is-to-be-known, and hence by description is unknown, and (ii) what is capable of being *known* only through the medium of a proposition, which, in turn (iii) in order to be a case of knowledge or be true, must correspond to the to-be-known, is to me the epistemological miracle. For the doctrine states that a proposition is true when it conforms to that which is not known save through itself. (1946:343)

From this point of view, contrary to what philosophers have assumed from the outset, the antecedently determinate can no more regulate the formation of our factual judgments than it can our judgments of value. But this is not to say that our judgments are therefore without measure, or that inquiry is indistinguishable from pure invention. To think this is precisely to fall into the trap that has ensnared the modern mind. Either our ideas are accurate re-presentations of what is already there or they are simply our own creations. Either we are dealing with a *conform* theory of truth and knowledge, or a *transform* theory,/5/ accept reality as the norm, or reduce the norm to one of personal satisfaction. As we have stressed from the beginning, there is another alternative and Dewey worked hard, though, to judge from his critics, with questionable success, to make that clear. Immediately after what I quoted above, he writes:

> My own view takes correspondence in the operational sense it bears in all cases except the unique epistemological case of an alleged relation between a "subject" and an "object"; the meaning, namely, of *answering*, as a key answers to conditions imposed by a lock, or as two correspondents "answer" each other; or, in general, as a reply is an adequate answer to a question or a criticism—as, in short, a *solution* answers the requirements of a *problem*. (1946:343)

Dewey is thus emphatically not rejecting any and every version of a *conform* theory of knowledge; he is simply denying that the relevant conformity is that of a picture or representation. Neither is he confusing "the three activities which, since the time of Aristotle, philosophers had sought to keep distinct, namely, *knowing, making* and *doing*" (Smith:85). Rather, he is saying that the *way* philosophers have tried to keep them distinct is a mistake. He is saying that there is no such thing as a disengaged, uninvolved, spectator-kind of knowing, no knowing that is a matter of simply "taking a look," no knowing that is not itself a function of making and doing. For Dewey, the process of inquiry along with its products, is essentially a transitional affair between two states of direct "having," i.e., between having things simply as given and having them as meaningful, between having them haphazardly and having them in such a way that intellect is at home with them. This is not to downgrade inquiry or the knowledge in which it terminates. It is simply to insist that knowledge is not something self-contained, that it arises and functions within a context and is significant by reason of its practical bearing on that context.

> The pragmatic theory of intelligence means that the function of mind is
> to project new and more complex ends—to free experience [by which Dewey
> means the inclusive affair of our common life] from routine and caprice. Not
> the use of thought to accomplish purposes already given either in the
> mechanism of the body or in that of the existent state of society but the use of
> intelligence to liberate and liberalize action, is the pragmatic lesson. (1917:63)

Inquiry therefore, and this means all inquiry, is primarily a practical, not a
theoretical affair. It is the transformation of our shared experience, our on-
going common life, into something more rich and meaningful. "Nothing,"
writes Dewey, "but the best, the richest and fullest experience possible, is
good enough for man" (1958:412). The only final end he would accept is
growth—growth in the meaningfulness of present experience. It is to this
end, an increase in the concrete sense and reasonableness of our lives, that
all of our activity should be directed. And it is to this end that the activity of
inquiry is undertaken, which means, of course, that the end of inquiry is
ultimately not the true, but the good (or, more precisely, *the better*), that
assertions of truth and falsity have their meaning not in themselves but in
their bearing on this quest for the good (a complete reversal of the perennial
position that the good is a function of the true,/6/ that right action is a
function of first knowing what is the case), and that, as essentially an effort
to determine what to do in the interest of greater meaningfulness (including,
e.g., what standrds to adopt for determining what is true), inquiry is
fundamentally and ultimately a deliberative enterprise. Dewey would agree
heartily with the following remark of another philosopher who insisted on
the priority of the practical question over the theoretical.

> In some sense, therefore, if we can act rightly it must be without a prior
> theoretical determination of what it is right to do. The discrimination of right
> and wrong in action must be prior to and not dependent upon the theoretical
> discrimination of the truth and falsity of a judgment. (Macmurray, 1957:141)

But Dewey would go a step further. He would also assert the converse; the
theoretical discrimination of truth or falsity presupposes and depends upon
the prior practical discrimination of right and wrong, of what makes more
sense and what doesn't. For the theoretical discrimination of truth and
falsity presupposes the availability of recognizably public standards and
criteria, which themselves have been previously fashioned in the interest of
more fruitful inquiry and so ultimately of greater sense. This is something
that cultural relativists or epistemological behaviorists seem to forget.
Bernstein writes:

> There is no other way to justify knowledge claims or claims to truth than
> by appealing to those social practices which have been hammered out in the
> course of human history and are the forms of inquiry *within* which we distin-
> guish what is true and false, what is objective and idiosyncratic. (762)

This "hammering out," however, has not been a random process. It has been a matter of deliberate judgment. These social practices, along with the norms and criteria inherent in them, were elaborated in function of man's quest for greater meaningfulness. They are not simply theoretical principles that happen to shape the way we inquire; they are tools that have been developed for a purpose, answers to an on-going question, and they can be *appraised as such*. It is thus the priority of man's practical quest for sense over whatever theoretical systems he may have devised in its pursuit that keep him finally from being imprisoned by them. In other words, we do more than simply employ the criteria at hand; we are also able to compare different systems and, in the light of the question to which they are answers, judge them as better or worse.

This, I suggest, has crucial significance for the matter in hand. For it provides a way of seeing philosophy's task as something other than the search for and grasp of ultimate truth. This has been the traditional approach. The philosopher's aim was to penetrate to an order of reality beyond the everyday, one on which the everyday could be seen to be based. It has been unabashedly foundational. Were there no such realm of metaphysical truth, not only would our everyday world be cut adrift in a sea of relativism but, perhaps more to be lamented, philosophers would have nothing to do. The view I have been developing shows this not to be the case. Philosophy's business is not the revelation of a deeper truth. In fact, its business is not directly with the true, or with what is the case at all, but with good. It is, you might say, the intellectual aspect of man's never-ending quest for sense.

What I mean is that, since man is capable of examining the norms and standards he has inherited in terms of their bearing on the shape of his life, it makes sense to do so. Customary standards of belief, conduct and appreciation were not developed reflectively and in relation to one another but more in response to existential needs. The result can be, and often is, a life that doesn't hang together as a whole, that is lived at cross purposes. What is required is a work of continual appraisal and criticism. The norms by which our life is shaped need to be evaluated as to their suitability to be such. This, I suggest, will give philosophers more than enough to do./7/ Instead of constructing ultimate world views which, despite their claims to the contrary, are more aesthetic than cognitive in character, more works of art than of knowledge (for they are reflective compositions which have been worked out in the light of that same interest in sense which guides all man's doings—and therefore, as Rorty remarks, not much better or worse than the ways of life they were supposed to ground), reconstructing this one should be their concern. In other words, not speculation but critical judgment, only here the judging looks to the overall sense of our common life and relates the item being appraised to its bearing on this as final value. The traditional view that philosophy has to do with reality as a whole is thus not mistaken.

The wholeness in question, however, is not, as has been thought, something antecedent to be cognitively grasped. Rather, the wholeness to which philosophy looks is one to be continually achieved, the comprehensive result of critically intelligent action.

4.

And so we come to the final item in the title of this paper: prayer. I have chosen to speak about prayer rather than about religious belief because of the priority of the practical question that I have been stressing. Often enough philosophers of religion take it as their main task to establish theoretically the existence of God. However, if the preceding remarks about the nature of philosophy are at all accurate, this emphasis is misplaced. The primary question is not: Does God exist? or, How can I know whether He does or not? The primary question from the point of view being developed in this paper is rather: How should I orient my life as a whole? Or better: What should I do for my life as a whole to make sense? This, after all, is the ultimate version of the practical question that underlies all of our doings./8/ And it is my contention that the practice of prayer provides the answer. Prayer, I will argue, is the ultimate form of right action and it is known to be right antecedent to the resolution of the theoretic issue of God's existence. In fact, prayer is the institution and maintenance of that context within which alone the very quest for sense can itself make sense. Let me explain.

We saw earlier how action as doing presupposes a context to which it is relevant, the context provided by the personal other with whom the agent stands in a relation of communication. What I want to say now is that for my life to be had as something whole, as making sense, that personal other must ultimately be conceived as one. If there is no One to whom I seek to be responsive in all my doings, then there is no way of binding these together. And since by these doings I define myself, so long as they remain radically many, my very selfhood is fragmented. As H. Richard Niebuhr put it:

> The self as one self among all the systematized reactions in which it engages seems to be the counterpart of a unity that lies beyond yet expresses itself in all the manifold systems of actions upon it. In religious language, the soul and God belong together; or otherwise stated, I am one within myself as I encounter the One in all that acts upon me. (122)

Or again:

> To respond to the ultimate action in all responses to finite actions means to seek one integrity of self amidst all the integrities of scientific, political, economic, educational, and other cultural activities; it means to be one responding self amidst all the responses of the roles being played, because there is present to the self the One other beyond all the finite systems of nature and society. (123)

Now, I would suggest that I *encounter* the One only if I invoke the One and the One is *present* only as invoked. The theistic interpretation of the other which is correlative to me at that point where, by my capacity to raise the practical question, I stand in judgment on all my empirical relationships, is not something that imposes itself willy-nilly or independently of that question. Rather, it presents itself as having a claim upon me only as implicit in the practical orientation which seems to be required for my life to be had as making sense (i.e., for the practical question to be finally and satisfactorily answered). Thus, if we take prayer to mean organizing one's life as a relation of invocation and response to a Transcendent You, then actually to intend sense unrestrictedly, i.e., actually to be bent on transforming one's life into something coherent and whole, is to experience prayer as something one ought to do. Conversely, not to pray is to find oneself lost in multiplicity. This is why there is a certain inevitability about the idea of God. The idea of God can be viewed as arising and being validated in the experience of prayer as alone making sense of life. This idea of God is, to be sure, an interpretative construct. But it is not a mere construct. It refers to the One disclosed in the unity and wholeness of our lives which prayer achieves and it must continually be refined and corrected in terms of that disclosure. In like manner, our praying itself needs continual evaluation in terms of the question to which it would be the final answer. Otherwise stated, a plausible case can be made for one conception of God as more adequate than another, for one way of praying as better than another and, in general, for one form of life as more human than another, because that radical quest for sense which man is provides a living and ultimate standard for appraising the various alternatives.

Thus we come back to the dominant theme of this paper. The idea that we can "know" what is better or worse only in relation to accepted standards but that the acceptance of these and the forms of life to which they are integral is ultimately arbitrary, is rooted in the more fundamental idea of reason as primarily theoretical. That conception sees man as a combination of infrarational, or at best nonrational, interests on the one hand, and a disinterested, purely cognitive reason on the other. It is this view which renders deliberation suspect, because according to it there are no norms that have not themselves been adopted, no norms that are not themselves open to question. If, however, there is an interest intrinsic to the very process of inquiry and at the basis of all rational activity the picture is radically changed. For as presupposed in every question, the practical interest in sense which is reason would be beyond question. It would provide a final standard of appraisal, a norm for evaluating all norms.

How this works out in various areas, I have tried to suggest. The important point to remember is that to identify reason with a radical and unrestricted appetite for a world that makes sense does not by itself settle any concrete issues. What it does is to provide a way of seeing rationality as fundamentally deliberative and to restore confidence in the possibility of man's reaching, at least in some cases, warranted judgments about what is worthwhile. In other words, by enabling man to view all the diverse systems he has elaborated for understanding and living in the world, not merely as a manifold of incompatible perspectives, but as various and more or less adequate answers to a universal question, it frees him from the paralyzing view that he is hopelessly submerged in one or another of these systems with no neutral standpoint from which to challenge it. This means that while no stand on how life should be lived can claim to be founded on the ultimate nature of things but will always be a matter of judgment, point at least is restored to rational discussion and argument. The merits and demerits of differing judgments can be meaningfully debated. And where the issue in question is the determination of our common world and the regulation of our common life, justice in place of power-struggles, the universally accept-able in place of whatever one may be able to get away with, become meaningful aims. Indeed if the idea of a universal community in which responsiveness to *You* is the supreme regulative principle and fellowship itself a cherished end—if such an idea can stir our hearts and evoke from us efforts to make it real, we have in the foregoing a basis for understanding why this should be so that does not at the same time preclude arguments to the contrary.

NOTES

/1/   Writing about the rationality of the basic postulates of scientific activity, Kecskemeti observes that "these postulates, as value standards, are not 'rational' because they are logically or empirically demonstrable; in fact, they are neither. Their rationality consists merely in their capacity to generate consensus, in a social situation, without recourse to suggestion and coercion" (318).

/2/   See Dewey's answer to Russell's criticism of his position in his essay "Propositions, Warranted Assertibility, and Truth" (1946:331–53).

/3/   See Dewey's remarks about the "controlling presence" of the indeterminate quality of the situation in his essay "Inquiry and Indeterminateness of Situations" (1946:322–30).

/4/   Macmurray expresses it this way: "Whatever [the agent] does is morally right if the particular intention of his action is controlled by a general intention to maintain the community of agents and wrong if it is not so controlled" (1961:119).

/5/   Smith uses this distinction, which he credits to A. P. Ushenko, *Power and Events* (Princeton University Press, 1946), to contrast the positions of Peirce, and to a lesser extent James, with that of Dewey. The *conform* theory "appeals to the authoritative force of an antecedent reality and requires the adjustment of thought to that reality; the [*transform* theory] rejects the antecedent reality, emphasizes the problematic or indeterminate character of the situation wherein thought is operative and aims at transforming that situation into a settled or determinate affair" (52).

/6/   A straightforward statement of what I have called the perennial position is found in Pieper's short study of Aquinas's doctrine on the virtue of prudence. He writes: "The pre-eminence of prudence means that realization of the good presupposes knowledge of reality" (25).

/7/   Some interesting insights in support of the thesis that the traditional conception of philosophy is an idea whose time has run out can be found in Raschke's "The End of Theology" and Picht's "The God of the Philosophers."

/8/   For the question "Does God exist?" Macmurray substitutes: "Is the universal Other, from which the community of persons distinguishes itself, and which is the same for all persons, a personal or impersonal Other?" (1961:215). This strikes me as still too dominantly theoretical and as presupposing the prior practical question: How should I relate myself to the universal Other, personally or impersonally?

WORKS CONSULTED

Bernstein, Richard J.
    1980   "Philosophy in the Conversation of Mankind." *Review of Metaphysics* 33:745–75.

Dewey, John
    1917   *Creative Intelligence: Essays in the Pragmatic Attitude.* New York: Henry Holt & Co.
    1938   *Logic: The Theory of Inquiry.* New York: Holt, Rinehart & Winston.
    1946   *Problems of Men.* New York: Philosophical Library.
    1958   *Experience and Nature.* New York: Dover Press.

Donagan, Alan
    1977   *The Theory of Morality.* Chicago and London: University of Chicago Press.

Kecskemeti, Paul
    1952   *Meaning, Communication, and Value.* Chicago: University of Chicago Press.

Kliever, Lonnie D.
    1977   "Authority in a Pluralistic World," *The Search for Absolute Values in a Changing World,* Vol. 1. *Proceedings of the Sixth International Conference on the Unity of the Sciences.* New York: International Culture Foundation Press, 157–173.

Macmurray, John
  1957   *The Self as Agent*. New York: Harper & Brothers.
  1961   *Persons in Relation*. New York: Harper & Brothers.

Margolis, Joseph
  1971   *Values and Conduct*. New York: Oxford University Press.

Niebuhr, H. Richard
  1963   *The Responsible Self*. New York: Harper & Row.

Picht, Georg
  1980   "The God of the Philosophers." *Journal of the American Academy of Religion* 48:61–79.

Pieper, Josef
  1959   *Prudence: The First Cardinal Virtue*. New York: Pantheon Books.

Raschke, Carl A.
  1978   "The End of Theology." *Journal of the American Academy of Religion* 46:159–79.

Rawls, John
  1971   *A Theory of Justice*. Cambridge: Harvard University Press.

Rorty, Richard
  1980   "Pragmatism, Relativism, and Irrationalism." *Proceedings and Addresses of the American Philosophical Association* 53:719–38.

Smith, John E.
  1978   *Purpose and Thought: The Meaning of Pragmatism*. New Haven: Yale University Press.

III.
Theology and the Moment
of Deconstruction

Metaphor and the Accession
to Theological Language

Charles E. Winquist

Mark the first page of the book with a red marker. For, in the beginning, the wound is invisible.   Reb Alce (Jabes:13)

Theology is writing. Sometimes it is implicit writing but it is always within the referential order of language. Religion is not always writing. The philosophy of religion is writing. Sometimes it is implicit writing but it is always within the referential order of language.

Theology and the philosophy of religion are related to religion and they are related to each other. It is easy to ascertain that their relationship to each other is semantic but their relationship to religion is enigmatic. Theology sometimes sees itself as religion and the philosophy of religion sometimes sees its relationship to theology as a relationship to religion. Theology seldom sees itself as religion without a remainder and the philosophy of religion usually recognizes this nonidentity. Whether the choice is to serve religion or to analyze it, it should be acknowledged at the beginning that neither philosophy nor theology can contain religion or fully substitute themselves for it. The enigmatic relationship of writing disciplines to religion is a reflection on writing and a reflection on religion.

Writing is repression. Theology is writing. Theology is repression. The philosophy of religion is writing. The philosophy of religion is repression. This means that the writing disciplines that are contiguous to religion are in their origin a repression of religion except in those instances when religion is itself writing.

The claim that accession to theological language is repression hinges on the two claims that writing is repression and that theology is writing. Neither claim is a direct result of theological thinking. Both result from thinking about thinking and are first drawn from the convergence of understanding in linguistics and psychoanalysis in describing meaning as representational. It is when writing becomes conscious of itself as representational that it refers back to itself as repression rather than as revelation.

The choice to focus on theological writing instead of theological speaking is an attempt to gain clarity in understanding the accession to theological language. When a text is spoken, it is often difficult to hear the text itself and not confuse it with the voice of the text. But that same text is capable of being written, and it is not incidental that language is capable of being written (Gadamer:354). In writing, the production of a text is disjoined from the organicity of speech-events because as a text it can stand by itself once it is written. It becomes a thing beside other things and is freed from the circumstances of origination. It no longer belongs to its author and the privacy of the author's intention. It resides among other texts in the referential order of language.

I do not mean to suggest that the organic complexity of speech and that the author's intention are unimportant and do not present hermeneutical problems; however, the examination of the abstract ideality of the text most easily isolated in writing gives us insight into language's functioning that can be obscured without this isolation.

First, the fact that the text can stand alone gives us a clue to the meaning of writing. Writing lifts experience into the referential order of language. Experience is transformed so that through a dialectic of presence and absence it is no longer identical with itself. Object language, written or spoken, evokes an object through the means of a substitute that is not the object. "The word is the presence of the thing it designates and posits it 'in itself' in its order of reality. Two separate but referential orders are thus ordered by the act of designation; the *real* and *language*" (Lemaire:51). In the realm of language the written text stands on a new stage and can be separated from author and original context. Even if we were to argue that the separation is a violation of the author's intention, it is still possible. This possibility is realized by the fact of the written text. The text has its own ontological status and can be evaluated as it presents itself.

Second, a written text presents itself in its own materiality. Phonetic elements are complemented by and sometimes displaced by pictographic and ideogrammatic elements that are not translatable into speech. This is particularly evident in hieroglyphic writings. The materiality of the written text can be likened to the steel or stone of the sculptor and the oils or acrylics of the painter although a difference must also be acknowledged. The likeness resides in the density of an ontological trace and the difference is in the ontic display of media dissimilarities. Ironically, the acknowledgement of a likeness is referential to Derrida's meaning of *differance* while the difference is determined amidst the material similarity of alternative media (1973:129–30). The combinant act of deferring, differing, and repeating creates and fills a space that is at once a presence and a representation. The presence is a representation of what is absent because of the deferring that is necessarily a differing. What is deferred is no longer present so that what is present differs from what is deferred.

Once a distinction is made between the order of the real and the order of language, most of us would like to cast our lot with the order of the real if we only could escape the bell jar that would descend upon this decision and silence its presence. The order of the real cannot even house cries or screams that are primitive representational presences once the real has been distinguished from the order of language. Language is a phenomenon in the order of the real only through the substance and texture of its own textuality. In the order of the real a cry is only a cry. It has meaning only in the order of language. When we appeal to referential determinations within this textual fabric we have entered the order of language.

We can speak or we can be silent. If we speak, our speech can be transformed into writing, and it then becomes difficult to deny that we have chosen to live within the order of language. Of course this is not an escape from the order of the real. First order experience belongs to the order of the real and the law of this house—the economics of force. The experience of experience belongs to the linguistic order and within this house we can talk about a semantics of meaning. This distinction is complicated by the recognition that although the experience *of* experience is described as being of a second order and within a semantics of meaning, as experience it is of the first order and also belongs to an economics of force. The semantics of meaning is itself overdetermined in an economics of force. There is an inside and an outside to second order experience and it is the inside that we are calling a semantics of meaning. Although the outside resides in what we mean from the inside by reality, whatever we know of the outside is known through the deployment of images on the inside. The epistemological dilemma is that what has an inside presence is an absence of the outside.

The populations of signs, words, and concepts within a semantics of meaning are present only to each other. The references are textual or intertextual. The text can be layered, but there is still no text but the present text (Derrida, 1978:211). This means that a consent to the givenness of experience insists on bracketing texts and seeing them in their own materiality. We surrender a natural attitude that naively identifies first and second order experience. We might want to say that the materiality of language intrudes upon the fantasy that direct experience is available to intelligence without being transformed by thinking. The economics of force is itself a concept within a semantics of meaning. This disjunction at the heart of our work appears to be an *aporia*, an impassable passage, that confronts us with the danger of a skeptical immobilization.

Theology accompanied by other writing disciplines often hesitates when this originating wound of thinking becomes visible. When the passage to primary experience is blocked by the nature of its own linguistic achievement, theology finds itself restricted to the space of this achievement. A semantic anxiety develops that has been described by Harold Bloom as an anxiety of influence (5–16). What he calls "the melancholy of the creative mind's desperate insistence upon priority" (13) and the need to "clear imaginative space" (5) for writing combine to form the problematic not only of modern poetry but also of theology. In the restricted space of linguistic presence we soon discover that the fundamental insight that texts refer to texts also means that behind theology there is only more theology. Our space is crowded by precursors and contemporaries and, unless theology can get to a source that is more primal than itself, new theology appears only to be a repetition or pedagogical tool.

The recent offspring of theological hesitations are expressions of methodological narcissism and obscurantist spiritualities. Both are disguises for theological thinking although in a more restricted space than that of the first hesitation. Positivistic withdrawals and declarations of the end of theology are repressions of tradition that first appear to clear a limited space. The clearing is illusory. By saying what theology cannot say, negative theologies live within the materiality of the tradition. The training for negative theology is positive theology since it shares in the materiality of the tradition. That is, declaring the end of theology is possible only because of the persistence of theology. It can even be said that the act of limiting theology is a theological writing contributing to the persistence of theology. The important contribution of negative theologies is that they demonstrate the vitality of theological thinking without the constraints of literalism but within the constraints of language. Negative theologies live with semantic anxiety and conserve the resources of the linguistic tradition even if they are unhappy within this constriction.

On the other hand, the appeal to primary experience in new spiritualities is usually little more than an abandonment of a rich linguistic tradition for an impoverished use of language in which the touch, sigh, or cry are substituted for more complex semantic constructions and bodily amplifications of feelings are substituted for more complex secondary experiences. The problem has not been solved. This denial of complexity is still within a semantics of meaning and is dependent upon image formation for its deployment. The appeal to feeling is representational and the references are to each other. There is still a presence that marks an absence. The impoverishment of the language of presence simply means that the experience of experience is a text with little texture.

A more familiar and traditional response to radical disjunctions between reality and meaning is the search for a new foundation or a return to originating experience. We can note these at the same time because the search for foundations is a synchronic fantasy reciprocating with the diachronic fantasy of a primal time outside of time. The discovery of a primal ground is to coincide with an effacement of history, an erasure of linguistic achievement leaving a *tabula rasa* ready for a reconstruction through fresh markings. In both examples the resolution of the *aporia* is thought to be possible through rigorous work. It is thought that the *aporia* has manifested itself because the thinking that crowds our space was inadequate or misguided. The underlying assumption is that we have encountered an *aporia* because we ventured down the wrong road. It is suggested that we need a new starting point and a new road. In its most naive expression, this quest begins with an assessment of semantic anxiety as an inappropriate response to what may be thought of as no more important than a category mistake. In its more critical expressions some sophisticated isomorphism between reality and language is transformed into a hypostasis of language. The trace of force is erased and we are left with a linguistic realism and sometimes a literalism. Ironically, the enfranchisement of language with the weight of a descriptive realism is a forgetfulness of language. What is absent is thought to be present and what is present is ignored.

When language convolutes and shows itself rather than feigning transparency to an objective world we sometimes see this as a failure of language. What we are experiencing is that language can stand independently of our individual consciousness once it is written. What is first thought to be a failure is better described as a wound and what is wounded is the claim that language follows consciousness and remains in its control. The subversion of consciousness through the distortion of language in the psychopathology of everyday life and the transcendence of consciousness in the revelatory power of language are exemplary displays of the dislocation of the subject from the controlling center of linguistic experience. The subject discovers itself as one object beside others in the linguistic achievement that marks the presence of the subject. This presence also reveals an absence. The epistemological dilemma becomes dressed in psychological meaning but is still a philosophical problem.

Foucault describes the problem as a loss of philosophical subjectivity. "The breakdown of philosophical subjectivity and its dispersion in a language that dispossesses it while multiplying it in the space created by its absence is probably one of the fundamental structures of contemporary thought" (42). The convolution of language, misshapen and craglike, "refers to itself and is folded back on a questioning of its limits" (Foucault:44). What language discovers is more language. It is this enclosure of language in a nondialectic semantic display that frustrates the return to origins or the search for foundations. Within the semantic order one metaphor is only substituted for another. The dialectic between force and meaning is conspicuous by its absence.

Ironically, subjectivity is lost in all attempts to fix its origins or foundations. It is given over to the referential interiority of the text. Subjectivity is not extinguished. It is simply displaced into the order of its own creation. Language becomes "the being-there of the mind" and "this 'reality of language' is nothing other than the meaning achieved by a behavior" (Ricoeur, 1970:384). Total reflection is impossible. Language can only mirror consciousness within the limited dimensionality of language. Total reflection is a concept that would dissolve the dialectical tension between force and meaning that is the first moment of its possibility. Limits to the achievement of consciousness are asymptotic to its extinction. Theology is not going to found itself in radical reflection. It is going to have to live in the tension of a crowded marketplace of ideas and language.

The great temptation of a postcritical theology is silence. The silence that can follow a critical hesitation is not a retreat but it is a goal that must be achieved. This would not be a simple achievement since we are already in language. In the recent work of Altizer we see just how complex it is to talk about a theological silence and paradoxically we find ourselves still speaking. He notes that silence is both the origin and end of speech (1977:4). It is the limit that we have encountered as a frustration to the quest for origins or foundations. The journey to the beginning and the journey to the end are indiscernible. We come to silence.

Altizer's active meditation on silence issues in an apocalyptic metaphor of total presence. This speaking of a total presence is a proleptic image exomorphic with the eschatological realization that it anticipates. The eschatological reality is silent and yet we keep on speaking. "Once speech has spoken its voice establishes a world or a field, and that field is indissoluble, it cannot simply disappear or pass away" (Altizer, 1977:16). He affirms that speech ends only at the dawning of a totally present actuality. The word could no longer be written, the extreme expression of the dialectic between force and meaning. This return to an origin that is also an end is not a return to the book but to the body.

Altizer continues to write. In the continuation of writing lies a clue to the meaning of theology. The metaphor of total presence is a negation. "Final presence can only have a negative identity to any integral or individual form of consciousness, therefore it will be wholly manifest to that consciousness as judgment, and as total judgment which consumes all given and individual identity" (Altizer, 1980:99).

Theology has been transgressive. It has been both prophetic and parabolic in its negation of a sedimented linguistic world. The salient characteristic evident in diverse prolix ruminations of systematic theologies or in the parabolic economies of theopoetics is the willingness to entertain language in an extreme distention of intelligibility bordering on silence. If we catalogue the tradition we continually stumble over images of the apocalypse, intimations of that than which nothing greater can be conceived, characteristic forms of angelic knowledge, rumors of ineffable meanings and other troped constructions within a semantics of meaning that wrestle with ordinary uses of language. When we have wrestled with whatever are our demons and are blessed with a new name, that name can be written and theology continues.

Theology does not cease to be transgressive. It is a work and not a solution. The deployment of eschatological formulae such as Altizer's total presence or

Anselm's supreme conceptuality are deconstructions of sedimented worlds of language. Theology is deconstructive of a crowded linguistic space in all of its creative moments and it is here that we see its future. It is our experience of language that describes a purpose for this activity. In particular, the accession to theological language is an explicit valuation of language turned against the achievement of a visible world of textual meanings. This turning against is also a receiving of the text. Tropes, transgressions, misreadings, misprision are all references to the word-event that describes the work of a deconstructivist hermeneutic. We engage ourselves with the theological tradition to make space for more theological thinking. It is the work and not the content of the work that is the first order theological achievement. It is the work that lives in the dialectic between force and meaning.

Speech and writing create a virtual space which is the possibility for a work of language. It is a space for unlimited reduplication and repetition. There are no limits on how many times language can fold on itself. In this sense its internal manifestation is unconditional. Foucault says that it is in this "virtual space where speech discovers the endless resourcefulness of its own image and where it can represent itself as already existing behind itself, already active beyond itself, to infinity" (55). It must be carefully noted that this fecundity is representational and in the semantic realm. This disclaimer, however, is an expression of the meaning of language acts and not a diminishment of their meaning. The celebration of poetic freedom is an acute consciousness of language itself. Language can reference itself in an unlimited display of possibilities. We accordingly come to enjoy meaning but we cannot ascertain that these fictions are concordant with the economy of forces that press round about this moment of freedom.

The reflection that enables us to elaborate the disjunction between meaning and force is an achievement within the realm of meaning that is exemplary of language turning on itself. Language determines within itself an indeterminate relationship to reality which is at the same time an expression of its reality. Language transcends the forces to which it indeterminately refers, but it cannot transcend itself. It can only subvert itself so that its transcendence of primary forces is compromised. The indeterminateness of this breaching is experienced as a loss of meaning within the semantic realm. Words and images are quickly deployed to cover the gap and the breach is then experienced as meaningful. It is of course no longer itself but a re-presentation. All that has been ascertained is that language and the semantics of meaning are not inclusive of reality but dwell in the neighborhood of nonlinguistic forces. This, however, is an important recognition from within language. It may be as close a rapprochement between the disjunctive realms of force and meaning as can be achieved within the realm of language. We cannot turn to the realm of force because its sense is mute until it is represented in language. The breaching of the disjunction only has meaning when it is reduplicated in the realm of language which is at the same time the reaffirmation of the disjunction. Whatever we mean by reality is always appearing and appearance.

Appearance or coming to appear is not sham or falsity. It is how experience comes to stand in speech and writing. The concept of appearance can also be an internal signifier of the closure of language as a system. As such it is an enigmatic concept because it has an indeterminate reference outside of itself. *Appearance* is an overdetermined concept and an indeterminate concept at the same time. It is overdetermined since it is connected not only to a semantics of meaning but also to the economics of force. It is indeterminate since the connection to the realm of force is a breaching that becomes meaningful only when it is represented in the semantics of meaning. Derrida speaks to this problem when he says, "Since language has not fallen from the sky, it is clear that the differences have been produced; they are effects produced, but effects that do not have as their cause a subject or substance, a thing in general, or a being that is somewhere and itself escapes the play of difference" (1973:141). He has defined the problem so that a closed system of language is experienced as incomplete. He then acknowledges that "I have tried to indicate a way out of the closure imposed by this system, namely, by means of the 'trace'. No more an effect than a cause, the 'trace' cannot of itself, taken outside of its context, suffice to bring about the required transgression" (1973:141). The path that he has indicated is still the path of language. The only possibility that he has shown as a way out of language is to follow the way of language.

The trace marks the breach and as such it is also a hinge. The trace would have no meaning without the breaching but the meaning of the breaching is determined only as it is deferred toward semantic representation. The appearance of the trace, that which gives it its difference in the semantic realm, is a sign of unresolved overdetermination. It is a lucid metaphor, a metaphor of metaphoricity. A lucid metaphor appears in terms of its metaphoricity. The hinge between the disjunctive realms of force and meaning must be metaphorical because it only has meaning as part of a semantic display. It is a metaphorical display of a metaphorical act. A similarity is discerned between dissimilar domains. The troping of a work within a text is layered over the breaching of the limits of textuality and appears in what is textually present as a coincidence of meaning. The similarity between what is dissimilar is only an apparent similarity; but this is no surprise since the meaning of a text is in its appearance. The "trace" appears and then disappears in a *mimesis* of its own metaphorical character. Its indeterminate meaning is substituted for its determinate meaning in a system of textual references and this is why it appears only to disappear.

The trace marks a fissure within language. It stops textual intrasignification from coming to complete expression. It is a momentary clearing within the work of language where we can pose the question of what lies beyond language. We are able to question, What have we forgotten? The trajectory of this question can be expressed but not contained within a semantics of meaning. The trace enfranchises the question of an extralinguistic reality and the scale of our inquiry has been altered. We need a different frame to attend to the importance of questions that violate the semantic framework in which they are enclosed. We need a place for language to "say" and "show" more than its internal content.

Ricoeur suggests that the movement to another framework is a shift from semantics to hermeneutics. He affirms that in a general theory of symbolism overdetermination refers to semantic and nonsemantic patterns of relationship. His concept of hermeneutics depends upon the fundamental condition "that symbolics is the means of expressing an extralinguistic reality. This is of the greatest importance for the subsequent confrontation; anticipating an expression which will take on its precise meaning only on another strategic level, I will say that in hermeneutics there is no closed system of the universe of signs" (Ricoeur, 1974:65).

Although I agree with Ricoeur that there is no closed system of the universe of signs, we should not confuse this claim with the hope for a symbolic realism that searches the contours of a semantics of meaning for nonsemantic symbols. The dilemma of semantic captivity is not that easily resolved. Within the realm of semantic meaning all that we will see is the text that presents itself. In the text the forces are present only as an absence. The symbol can reside in a semantic text only as a metaphor and we can talk about an extralinguistic reference only if it is a lucid metaphor. Even then it is language referencing its own nature.

The notion of the symbol is developed within language and marks a point around which language can turn or fold on itself. It is in this second order of reflexivity that the symbol is mirrored as a lucid metaphor. The need for a hermeneutical framework is secondarily derived from the symbol but primarily derived from the lucid metaphor. This is just one of the peculiar qualities of language when it folds and mirrors itself. We are still within language, and I have focused on the shift from symbol to metaphor to emphasize that hermeneutics is implied by the metaphoricity of language.

Language—the presence of an absence—is metaphorical by its very deployment. It substitutes meaning for force. Marking the similarity of the dissimilar realms of force and meaning can only be an achievement of metaphor. The force disappears paradoxically in the substitution that constitutes its appearance in a realm of meaning. This means that the lucidity of the metaphor is only self-referential. It reveals its own nature but not the nature of the forces that have disappeared. Force is repressed as force to be revealed as meaning.

Hermeneutics is a work and movement in language that turns language on itself. We can best understand its importance if we contrast its movement with the first order of a semantic achievement. The semantic achievement of language is to bring force to meaning. This work is a transformation and a repression. Meaning is substituted for force and what we hold in consciousness is meaning. In contrast, hermeneutics as we have conceived it brings meaning to force. This is a movement and not a transformation. It remains within the semantic realm. Force is not substituted for meaning. What we hold in consciousness is meaning. However, our hold has become tenuous. The meaning that we hold onto is metaphorical. The meaning of meaning, language folded on itself, brings us to the recognition of the absence which is present as the achievement of language. Meaning is brought to force, gives recognition to force, but does not become force. We come to dwell at the foundation of conscious meaning without surrendering consciousness. The lucid metaphor in its indeterminateness is especially permeable to the forces of origination that language brings to meaning. We might at this point say that the critical violence of hermeneutical inquiry releases consciousness from its sedimented achievement by self-inflicted wounds that are at the same time openings for the transformation of force into meaning. Forces are freshly reduplicated in a metaphorical deployment. A postcritical text is formed.

We begin to understand why theology fashioned as a hermeneutical movement must be transgressive. The hermeneutical task is not the exegesis of a precritical or postcritical text. Exegesis is another task that has been traditionally assumed by theology in the complexification and sedimentation of meaning. It has a linear function in the extention of meaning which is also a further sedimentation. The hermeneutical exigency appears when language is forced back on itself in the crowded marketplace of ideas. When the reflexive wound appears, hermeneutical thinking takes on a special urgency because we are acutely conscious that exegesis is a textual repetition that solidifies the repression of primal forces. Force is deferred in systematic differentiation until hermeneutics turns the achievement of language around toward its metaphorical origin.

The hermeneutical exigency as we have defined it is not felt until language reflects on itself after its first level of achievement has languished in a commonplace familiarity increasingly crowded with new linguistic formulations but forgetful of forces that it has brought to meaning. What is first sometimes thought to be a loss of meaning is better described as a loss of the meaning of meaning. That is, when language does not see itself mirrored as a metaphorical achievement it becomes flattened in a horizontal semantic display. It is dazzled by the complexity of what is present and forgets that the presence reveals an absence. The loss of that sense of absence negates consciousness of the achievement of language as a transformation of force into meaning.

The sense of absence attends every experience of the experience of language. The hermeneutical exigency is satisfied in the consciousness of the sound of silence and the presence of absence. It is this consciousness that is at once both hermeneutical and theological. The lucid metaphor appears and is attended to in the radical questions of hermeneutical thinking that can be descriptively characterized as an accession to theological language or the theological use of language. Not only is the language of a wholly other absence often part of a theological lexicon but the entertainment of unconditional questions is itself a theological inquiry. Theology can push language to limits of intelligibility where ordinary meanings are prophetically negated or parabolically reversed. There are two transgressions. When concepts transgress the limits of intelligibility in extreme formulations, their meaning disappears. We are then conscious not of present meaning but of the disappearance of meaning into an absence that now is itself only a memory. The other transgression is turning language on itself in a parabolic reversal that wounds established external meanings. This self-referential moment is a display of the materiality or metaphoricity of language. That is, when language turns on itself it encounters a presence that is no more than itself. The parabolic reversal is an acute consciousness of absence. The metaphor gains in lucidity. Meaning is brought closer to force by the recognition of what language is and what it is not. In act and content this recognition is a theological affirmation because in all of its expressions it intends the theological silence that is both absent and other than itself.

Force is a reality other than language (Derrida, 1978:27). Consciousness thus transcends the achievement of its linguistic display in the struggle for origination. This wrestling with unnamed demons may issue forth in theological meaning but it is first of all an experience of transcendence that is religious. The postcritical text is now also in its fresh statement a precritical text. The theological and hermeneutical exigencies have led us to force and thereby to religion.

Theology is not force and theology is not religion. Theology is writing and writing is repression. Unless it becomes silent, theology can always return to the book, to writing. Theology is a pretext. Its hermeneutical achievement is writing; but this is a pretext. It is only when we know that it is a pretext that we know about its work and at the same time know that its work is not what it is about.

From a conversation in a novel by Kazantzakis (69) we see into a situation and into an intention that must parallel our own situation and intention in theological thinking.

> "I've been working out a big plan in my mind these last few days, a crazy idea. Is it on?"
> "Need you ask me? That's what we came here for: to carry ideas into effect."
> Zorba craned his neck, looked at me with joy and fear.
> "Speak plainly boss!" he cried. "Didn't we come here for the coal?"
> "The coal was a pretext, just to stop the locals being too inquisitive, so that they took us for sober contractors and didn't greet us by slinging tomatoes at us. Do you understand Zorba?"

> Zorba was dumbfounded. He tried hard to understand: he could not
> believe in such happiness. All at once, he was convinced. He rushed towards
> me and took me by the shoulders.
> "Do you dance?" he asked me intensely. "Do you dance?"

If we speak plainly about theology, we will have to say that the content of theology is a pretext for doing theology, and we can do theology until we are silent.

WORKS CONSULTED

Altizer, Thomas J. J.
  1977   *The Self-Embodiment of God.* New York: Harper & Row.
  1980   *Total Presence: The Language of Jesus and the Language of
                  Today.* New York: Seabury Press.

Bloom, Harold
  1973   *The Anxiety of Influence: A Theory of Poetry.* New York:
                  Oxford University Press.

Derrida, Jacques
  1973   *Speech and Phenomena.* Evanston: Northwestern University
                  Press.
  1978   *Writing and Difference.* Chicago: University of Chicago Press.

Foucault, Michel
  1977   *Language, Counter-Memory, Practice.* Ithaca: Cornell Univer-
                  sity Press.

Gadamer, Hans Georg
  1975   *Truth and Method.* New York: Seabury Press.

Kazantzakis, Nikos
  1952   *Zorba the Greek.* New York: Simon and Schuster.

Lemaire, Anika
  1979   *Jacques Lacan.* London, Henley, and Boston: Routledge &
                  Kegan Paul Ltd.

Ricoeur, Paul
  1970   *Freud and Philosophy: An Essay on Interpretation.* New
                  Haven: Yale University Press.
  1974   *The Conflict of Interpretations.* Evanston: Northwestern Uni-
                  versity Press.

G N I C A R T
T R A C I N G
Inter Alios

Mark C. Taylor

1.

Trace: A visible mark or sign of the former presence or passage of some person, thing, or event; vestige, track, trail. To follow the footprints of. To copy by following the lines of the original drawing on a transparent sheet placed upon it. To plait, twine, interweave.

Tracing: Drawing. Dancing. Following, *Imitatio*. Interweaving: one becoming two, or three, or . . . , while remaining one. An identity-in-difference and a difference-in-identity.

2.

To trace is to follow, copy, imitate, represent. Tracing represents by forming an image, an *imago* which is both identical with and different from the traced. Representation presents by absenting and absents by presenting. Tracing, therefore, simultaneously reveals and conceals the origin-al.

3.

If trace is vicar, then representation is vicarious satisfaction—sublation is sublimation.

4.

"The presence-absence of the trace . . . carries in itself the problems of the letter and the spirit, of body and soul. . . . All dualisms, all theories of the immortality of the soul or of the spirit, as well as all monisms, spiritualist or materialist . . . are the unique theme of a metaphysics whose entire history was compelled to strive toward the reduction of the trace."

○ ○ ○ ○ ○

5.

Our task is to undo the theology of presence and the philosophy of absence with a hermeneutics of word. The theology of identity and the philosophy of difference join in a philosophical theology and theological philosophy of identity-in-difference and difference-in-identity.

6.

"Dialectics is apocalypse; reversal; wakening from the dead."
.Noisrevnoc si hcihw noisrevni eht si noisiv citpylacopa

7.

The principle of noncontradiction is the cross upon which Albion hangs. "The Pentecostal darkness: the sun shall be turned to darkness. To overcome the opposition of darkness and light, cleanliness and dirt, order and chaos; the marriage of heaven and hell. To seduce the world to madness. Christ is within the wall of paradise, which is the wall of the law of contradiction; and the destruction of the law of contradiction is the supreme task of higher logic."

8.

Identity *is* difference and difference *is* identity. "In other words, identity is the reflection-into-self that is identity only as internal repulsion, and is this repulsion as reflection-into-self, repulsion which immediately takes itself back into itself. Thus it is identity as difference that is identical with itself. But difference is only identical with itself in so far as it is not identity but absolute non-identity. But non-identity is absolute in so far as it contains nothing of its other but only itself, that is, in so far as it is absolute identity with itself. Identity, therefore, is *in its own self* absolute non-identity. But it is also the *determination* of identity as against non-identity. . . . Difference in itself is self-related difference; as such it is the negativity of itself, the difference not of an other, but *of itself from itself*; it is not itself but its other. But that which is different from difference is identity. Difference is therefore itself and identity. Both together constitute difference; it is the whole, and its moment."

9.

Otherness is not merely other, difference is not indifferent. "Apart from the self-embodiment of otherness, identity could not stand out from itself, hence self-identity would be neither manifest nor actual. Nor can self-identity appear and be real apart from identity's own embodiment in otherness."

10.

Seeing the yes in the no and the no in the yes is the discovery that affirmation is negation and negation is affirmation. "The determinations which constitute the positive and negative consist . . . in the fact that the positive and negative are . . . absolute *moments* of the opposition; their subsistence is inseparably *one* reflection; it is a single mediation in which each *is* through the non-being of its other, and so *is* through its other or its own non-being. . . . In the first place, then, each *is, only in so far as the other is*; it is what it is, through the other, through its own non-being; it is only a *positedness*; secondly, it is, *in so far as the other is not*; it is what it is, through the non-being of the other; it is *reflection-into-self*. But these two are the *one* mediation of the opposition as such, in which they are simply only *posited moments.*"

11.

Nihilism is the inability to see positivity in negativity, presence in absence. Dogmatism is the inability to see negativity in positivity, absence in presence. Vision is the ability to see positivity in negativity and negativity in positivity, presence in absence and absence in presence.

12.

You cannot name God without naming Satan. Satan is called Opacity; God, Transparency.

13.

To see is to see into; genuine sight is always in-sight. To see into is to see through, through to the indwelling other. "Here, every given identity must pass into its own intrinsic opposite, must become its own inherent other, if apocalyptic reversal is to occur. Such a reversal is not a literal negation of the reality which it affects, it is rather a total transformation of the meaning and actuality of that reality, thereby allowing it to evolve into a wholly new form and identity."

14.
A(R)MO(U)R

The agony of identity and difference is host-ility. "Our enemy our host who feeds us." *Corpus Mysticum: Parasitos* and *Hostia* joined in Holy Communion. *Hoc est corpus meum.* Hocus-pocus: hostility becomes love. "Eucharist is the marriage feast; the union of the bridegroom and the bride." The wedding of identity and difference is the hierogamy which is hierophantic.

※ ※ ※ ※

15.

A trace is a mark; Mark, a trace. Tracing is marking; Marking, tracing. ". . . the self of the living present is primordially a trace."

16.

"Beneath the bottoms of the Graves, which is Earth's
        central joint,
There is a place where Contrarieties are equally true . . ."

17.

"Selving"

"I am the strife
    For the strife is just this conflict,
        Which is not any indifference of the two as diverse,
    But is their being bound together.
I am not the one of these two
    Taking part in the strife,
        But am both the combatants
    And the strife itself.
I am the fire and the water
    Which touch one another . . .
        The collision and the unity of what flies apart . . .
    Of what is now separated,
                        Fragmented,
And now is reconciled in unity with itself."

18.

Selfhood is *agon*, selving agony. Selves struggle to join the opposites they are. The more vital the self, the deeper the opposites. Contradiction is the universal life-pulse.

19.

The self is "a relation which relates itself to its own self, and in relating itself to its own self, relates itself to another"—an other within and an other without. Relation to the other within turns everything upside down, and the relation to the other without turns everything inside out. Upside down and inside out: madness—or salvation.

20.

Instead of "to be *or* not to be," the sum of the matter is to be *and* not to be, for to be is not to be, and not to be is to be. "Let those who insist that being and nothing are different tackle the problem of stating in what the difference consists." My identity *is* my difference, and my difference *is* my identity.

21.

"Now presence becomes absence, and becomes actual as absence, and that absence is the self-enactment of presence. Therefore presence can now be actual only in its absence, in its absence from itself, from its own self-identity." My presence *is* an absence, and my absence *is* a presence.

22.

Question: "Have you noticed that only in time of illness or disaster or death are people real?"
Answer: Death is the absence in the presence of which the self becomes itself.

23.

A fundamental theological puzzle for our time:

Is   ◯   empty or full?

Bindu: zero *or* semen; zero *and* semen.

Nada and *Niente* derive from *Nasci*.

o o o o o

24.

The question is no longer how the Word redeems, but how to redeem the Word.

25.

Optical Allusions: Hieroglyphics as Hierophany

Ground grounds figure—figure turns from and returns to ground. Only so is figure ground-ed. Yet a figureless ground is groundless. Ground, therefore, is figural. Figure grounds ground. Figure(s) ground(s) figure(s) ground(s) figure(s) ground(s) . . .

26.

"The relation of ground and grounded becomes an external form imposed on the content which is indifferent to these determinations. But in point of fact the two are not external to one another; for the content is this, to be the *identity* of the *ground* with itself in the *grounded*, and of the *grounded* in the *ground*. The side of the ground has shown that it is itself a posited, and the side of the grounded that it is itself ground; each is in itself this identity of the whole."

27.

White space is the emptiness which surrounds and invades the word. Without white
space, there is only darkness, invisibility.
Black space is the fullness which surrounds
and invades the wordless. Without dark
space, there is only light, invisibility.
Word reveals the fullness of emptiness and
the emptiness of fullness. Writing is
scripture, the play, or the interplay of
white space and black space which
enlightens by bringing darkness to light
and light to darkness. Words or Golgotha.

28.

The negative is positive and the positive is negative.

29.

"To say that madness is dazzlement is to say that the madman sees the
daylight, the same daylight as the man of reason (both live in the same
brightness); but seeing this same daylight, and nothing but this daylight and
nothing in it, he sees it as void, as night, as nothing; for him the shadows are
the way to perceive daylight. Which means that, seeing the night and the
nothingness of the night, he does not see at all. And believing he sees, he
admits as realities the hallucinations of his imagination and all the multitud-
inous population of the night. That is why delirium and dazzlement are in a
relation which constitutes the essence of madness, exactly as truth and light,
in their fundamental relation, constitute classical reason."

30.

"Is not the body's erotic zone where the garment leaves gaps?" The
textuality of sexuality.

31.

"Dreams attest that we constantly mean something other than what we
say; in dreams the manifest meaning endlessly refers to hidden meaning;
that is what makes every dreamer a poet. From this point of view, dreams

express the private archeology of the dreamer, which at times coincides with
that of entire peoples. . . . The analyst interprets this account, substituting
for it another text which is, in his eyes, the thought-content of desire, i.e.,
what desire would say could it speak without restraint." The sexuality of
textuality.

32.

Language games: Language is a game—we the players. We play the
game and the game plays us. But what kind of a game is this? It is a game
of hide-and-seek. Who, then, is it? Rather what is it, es, id?

33.

Homo linguisticus: We make the game and the game makes us.
Making it and being made. Playing the game, we play with ourselves.
Language is autoerotic—masturbation. *Homo linguisticus* is *Homo* homo.
Be careful not to get caught when you are playing hide-and-seek. Daddy
will cut id off, or tell you to be silent. Wait until Abba is gone to play.
Speech comes when "Nobodaddy" is gone—He is dead when word(s) come.

34.

Logos Spermatikos: Semen-ial, seminary words to be dis-seminated. The
flow of creative juices. "The word *cerebral* is from the same root as Ceres,
goddess of cereals, of growth and fertility; the same root as *cresco*, to grow,
and *creo*, to create. Onians, archaeologist of language, who uncovers lost
worlds of meaning, buried meanings, has dug up a prehistoric image of the
body, according to which head and genital intercommunicate via the spinal
column: the gray matter of the brain, the spinal marrow, and the seminal fluid
are all one identical substance, on tap in the genital and stored in the head."
White be-coming gray be-coming black. Penis as pen and pen as pen-is.

35.

[W]rite: The *arche* of forgetting is fore-getting. The *telos* of remembering is re-membering. Ritual enacts a play of forgetting and remembering.
On the one hand, rituals are necessary because we forget, possible because
we remember. On the other hand, rituals are necessary because we remember, possible because we forget. Writual is the dramatic struggle to present
the absent and to absent the present.

36.

"To make in ourselves a new consciousness, an erotic sense of reality, is to become conscious of symbolism. Symbolism is mind making connections (correspondences) rather than distinctions (separations). Symbolism makes conscious interconnections and unions that were unconscious and repressed. Freud says, symbolism is on the track [is a trace] of a former identity, a lost unity: the lost continent, Atlantis, underneath the sea of life in which we live enisled; or perhaps even our union with the sea (Thalassa); oceanic consciousness; the unity of the whole cosmos as one living creature, as Plato said in the *Timaeus.*"

37.

Spacing is a caesurean birth. "Trace is the opening of the first exteriority in general, the enigmatic relationship of the living to its other and of an inside to an outside: spacing."

38.

Blanks, gaps, holes are not empty, but are full, whole, holey. "Between the letters and the lines, and all around the blank margins, the spirit circulates freely. . . ."

39.

Satan is called Opacity, God is named Transparency. "Transparency. To let the light not on but in or through. To look not at the thing but through it; to see between the lines; to see language as lace, black on white; or white on black as in the sky at night, or in the space on which dreams are traced."

o   o   o   o   o

40.

Silence is the white space, voice the black space of speech. "In a dialectical view: silence and speech, these two, are one."

41.

"The silence of silence comes to an end in the presence of speech, as the actuality of speech shatters silence, embodying in its pure otherness a silence which is the other of itself. Silence cannot simply be silent in the presence of speech, for silence speaks in the voice of speech, and speaks in that self-negating otherness which embodies itself in its own otherness. Silence as silence is absent in speech, but silence is present as the 'other' of speech, and in that presence it embodies a new identity of itself."

42.

If *nothing* can be said, then how can we hear the unsaid? "A raid on the inarticulate" can be mounted only if nothing *can* be said.

43.

Silenus, leader of the satyrs, is the foster-father of Bacchus. Silence is the Bacchanalian revel which awakens the dreamer from "Newton's sleep" to twofold, threefold, fourfold vision.

44.

To hear silence is to see gaps. The prophet and the analyst know that for those who have ears to hear and eyes to see, there is no literal truth. "To let the silence in is symbolism."

o   o   o   o   o

45.

"The meaning is not in the words but between the words, in the silence; forever beyond the reach, the rape, of literal-minded explication; forever inviolate, forever new; the still unravished bride of quietness. The virgin womb of the imagination in which the word becomes flesh is silence; and she remains a virgin."

46.

Meaning is relative or relational. It arises from the play, the interplay of identity and difference, presence and absence, light and darkness, voice and silence.

47.

If, as the poet claims, "Things are because of interrelations, interactions," then "Meaning is not in things but in between; in the iridescence, the interplay; in the interconnections; at the intersections, at the crossroads. Meaning is transitional as it is transitory; in the puns or bridges, the correspondence."

48.

"Dans la langue il n'y a que des differences sans termes positifs." In other words "As far as a language is concerned, it is the lateral relation of one sign to another which makes each of them significant, so that meaning appears only at the intersection of and as it were in the interval between words." Meaningful intercourse.

49.

The contextuality of meaning and the meaningfulness of context disclose the texture of texts. Texts are fabric-actions woven from texts. The warp and woof of textual interweaving is tracing.

o o o o o

50.

A design: To de-sign

"To design is to cut a trace. Most of us know the word 'sign' only in its debased meaning—lines on a surface. But we can make a design also when we cut a furrow into the soil to open it to seed and growth. The design is the whole of the traits of that drawing which structures and prevails throughout the open, unlocked freedom of language. The design is the drawing of the being of language, the structure of a show in which are joined the speakers and their speaking: what is spoken and what of it is unspoken in all that is given in the speaking."

51.

Dialectical reversal turns inside out and outside in. Subject and object are inseparably bound in a relation of coimplication in which each becomes itself through the other. To know, therefore, is "to have the outside inside and to be inside the outside."

52.

In poetic language, the universe of discourse *becomes* the discourse of the universe. According to Malraux, Renoir's "vision was less a way of looking at the sea than the secret elaboration of a world to which that depth of blue whose immensity he was recapturing pertained."

53.

Vision is synesthetic: a seeing which is a saying and a saying which is a seeing.

54.

To hear the Word is to see. "The parables of Jesus are circumspections of the horizon or horizons of things. This is the reason the details of the narrative picture, though set out with intense realism, cannot be pressed: they invite attention, not to themselves, but to the horizon, just as the painting leads our eye unfalteringly to the vanishing point [i.e., the *bindu*]. Of the painting, for instance, the animals painted on the walls of Lascaux, Merleau-Ponty writes: 'It is more accurate to say that I see according to it, or with it, than that I *see it*.' The parable and the painting draw the eye, by means of a skillfully arranged soft focus on objects in the foreground, to the horizon by virtue of which those objects gain their places and faces. Thus, the objects in the foreground previously released again become the object of attention, but within a new horizon and undergirded and protected by fresh integrity."

o o o o o

55.

Metaphor is a cross—of identity and difference, presence and absence, voice and silence. Metaphorical vision is *stereopsis*: seeing identity-in-difference and difference-in-identity, pluralized unity and unified plurality. To see metaphorically is to become cross-eyed.

56.

"In order that a metaphor obtains, one must continue to identify the previous incompatibility *through* the new compatibility [Transparency]. 'Remoteness' is preserved within 'proximity.' To see *the like* is to see the same in spite of, and through, the different. This tension between sameness and difference characterizes the logical structure of likeness."

57.

The category of "metaphor" is neither noetic nor ontological, but is onto-noetic. "Metaphor and symbol serve to carry over into consciousness the carrying over between things, and between things and the self, in their very being."

58.

A metaphysics of metaphor is a metaphysics of "final participation" whose object is to object to the object, without being subject to the subject.

59.

Metaphor is born of that higher logic which shatters the law of noncontradiction. "Logic is only slavery within the bounds of language. Language has within it, however, an illogical element, the metaphor. Its principal force brings about an identification of the nonidentical; it is thus an operation of the imagination."

60.

As transitional language μεταφωρά carries the old over to the new, and speaks the new through the old. Thus the metaphor conceals even while revealing, and reveals even while concealing. Metaphorical language is always "*sous rature.*"

61.

Jesus   ✕   God.

62.

Metaphor is the language of the frontiersman, the path-finder who seeks the trail, searches the traces which lead from this world to the next. "One should meditate upon all of the following together: writing as the possibility of the road and of difference, the history of writing and the history of the road, of the rupture, of the *via rupta*, of the path that is broken, beaten, *fracta*, of the space of reversibility and of repetition traced by the opening, the divergence from, and the violent spacing of nature, of the natural, savage, salvage, forest. The *silva* is savage, the *via rupta* is written, discerned, and inscribed violently as the difference, as form imposed on the *hyle*, in the forest, in wood as matter. . . ."

63.

"In an *Ndembu* ritual context, almost every article used, every gesture employed, every song or prayer, every unit of space and time, by convention stands for something other than itself. It is more than it seems, and often a good deal more. The Ndembu are aware of the expressive or symbolic function of ritual elements. A ritual element or unit is called *chijikijilu*. Literally, this word signifies a 'landmark' or 'blaze.' Its etymon is *ku-jikijila*, 'to blaze a trail'—by slashing a mark on a tree with an ax or breaking one of its branches. This term is drawn originally from the technical vocabulary of hunting, a vocabulary heavily invested with ritual beliefs and practices. *Chijikijilu* also means a 'beacon,' a conspicuous feature of the landscape, such as an ant hill, which distinguishes one man's gardens or one chief's realm from another's. Thus, it has two main significations: (1) as a *hunter's blaze* it represents an element of connection between known and unknown territory, for it is by a chain of such elements that a hunter finds his way back from the unfamiliar bush to the familiar village; (2) as both *blaze* and *beacon* it conveys the notion of the structured and ordered as against the unstructured and chaotic. Its ritual use is already metaphorical: it connects the known world of sensorily perceptible phenomena with the unknown and invisible realm of the shades. It makes intelligible what is mysterious, and also dangerous."

64.

Metaphor is blaze, fire—"Apocalypse Now"—realized eschatology. The apocalyptic world is the world of "total metaphor." For the seer, "The whole creation will be consumed and appear infinite and holy, whereas it now appears finite and corrupt."

65.

Parable is "expanded metaphor," "the linguistic incarnation." Παρα βολή: "'Para' is a double antithetical prefix signifying at once proximity and distance, similarity and difference, interiority and exteriority, something inside a domestic economy and at the same time outside it, something simultaneously this side of a boundary line, threshold, or margin, and also beyond it, equivalent in status and also secondary or subsidiary, submissive, as of guest to host, slave to master. A thing in 'para', moreover, is not only simultaneously on both sides of the boundary line between inside and out. It is also the boundary itself, the screen which is a permeable membrane connecting inside and outside. It confuses them with one another, allowing the outside in, making the inside out, dividing them and joining them. It also forms an ambiguous transition between one and the other."

66.

Parable: "an ambiguous transition between one and another." The parable projects a world into which it attempts to translate the hearer. "Since the world it describes deforms the 'received' world, it constitutes nothing less than an invitation to live in that world, to see the world in that way, to take up one's abode within a totality of significations that is different from the everyday world."

67.

Reading a parable, therefore, is a *meta phora*, a passage, a journey a pilgrimage. *Imitatio*: to follow the footprints of.

68.

"One is inside
then outside what one has been inside,
One feels empty
because there is nothing inside oneself
One tries to get inside oneself
    that inside of the outside
    that one was once inside
    once one tries to get oneself inside what
    one is outside:
    to eat and to be eaten
to have the outside inside and to be
    inside the outside."

69.

As "visible inclusions of the alien in the sight of the familiar," metaphors and parables are imaginative without being imaginary. "Resemblance in metaphor is an activity of the imagination; and in metaphor the imagination is life."

70.

Imagination is the power of life and death—the means by which the absent becomes present and the present becomes absent.

71.

"Then Jesus appeared standing by Albion as the Good Shepherd
By the lost Sheep that he had found, & Albion knew that it
Was the Lord, the Universal Humanity; & Albion saw this Form
A Man, & they conversed as Man with Man in Ages of Eternity.
And the Divine Appearance was the likeness & similitude of Los."

72.

"God and the imagination are one."

73.

Metaphors and parables are stumbling-blocks to Jews and folly to Greeks.
Only Frontiersmen, limen, magicians, passengers, and madmen speak in metaphors and parables. "It is for the other world that the madman sets sail in his
fools' boat; it is from the other world that he comes when he disembarks. The
madman's voyage is at once a rigorous diversion and an absolute Passage. In
one sense, it simply develops across a half-real, half-imaginary geography, the
madman's liminal position on the horizon of medieval concern—a position
symbolized and made real at the same time by the madman's privilege of being
confined within the city *gates*; his exclusion must enclose him; if he cannot and
must not have another *prison* than the *threshold* itself, he is kept at the point of
passage. He is put in the interior of the exterior, and inversely. A highly
symbolic position, which will doubtless remain his until our own day, if we are
willing to admit that what was formerly a visible fortress of order has now
become the castle of our conscience."

74.

Madness. And yet, "there is no nonmetaphoric language to oppose to
metaphors."

75.

"The antinomy between mind and body, word and deed, speech and
silence, overcome. Everything is only a metaphor; there is only poetry."
o o o o o

76.

Poetry puts magic back into words. "Poetry is the establishment of
Being by means of the word."

77.

POIESIS
"By the word of the Lord the heavens were made,
    and all their host by the breath of his mouth.
For he spoke, and it came to be;
    he commanded, and it stood forth."

78.

```
A B R A C A D A B R A
A B R A C A D A B R
A B R A C A D A B
A B R A C A D A
A B R A C A D
A B R A C A
A B R A C
A B R A
A B R
A B
A
```

Abracadabra, the magic word which discloses the magic of words, probably derives from Abraxas. $a+\beta+\rho+a+\xi+a+s = 365$.

79.

Abraxas: *Ab ben rouach hakados; soteria apo xylou* (Father, Son, Spirit, Holy; Salvation from the cross); or *Anthropous sozon hagioi xyloi* (Saving mankind by the holy cross).

80.

The "Good Shepherd" who is the "shepherd of Being" is a "word magician." "The clearest evidence of Jesus' knowledge and use of magic is the eucharist, a magical rite of a familiar sort."

81.

The true magician crosses homeopathic and contagious magic, the metaphoric and the metonymic, the paradigmatic and the syntagmatic,

```
            S
            Y
            N
            C
    DIACHRONIC
            R
            O
            N
            I
            C
```

Magic is the union of time and eternity, "the marriage of heaven and hell."
"The bird fights its way out of the egg. The egg is the world. Who would be
born must first destroy a world. The bird flies to God. That God's name is
Abraxas. . . . Abraxas was the god who was both god and devil." "Fearful
symmetry."

o o o o o

82.

A metaphor for metaphor: *Word*.

83.

We must begin with absence, with silence, with the confession of the
absence of word(s). And we must dwell with this silence until we can hear,
hear how absence presents. Then we shall see, see that the word is absent
when present, and present when absent.

84.

The Road to Emmaus
When Jesus was present, he was absent, when absent, present. Why?
Because he is Word.

On the road to Emmaus, Jesus' presence is absence, and his absence is
presence. They see, but do not see; they hear only the silence of an empty
tomb. "And when he had sat down with them at the table, he took bread
and said the blessing; he broke the bread, and offered it to them. Then their
eyes were opened, and they recognized him; and he vanished from their
sight." *Hoc est corpus meum*. Hocus-pocus: a vanishing act that really
opened their eyes! And what do they see? They see his presence in absence.
But to do so, they must likewise see absence in their presence. To hear the
Word is to see, to see the presence in absence which answers our absence in
presence.

85.

"Dialectics is apocalypse, reversal; wakening from the dead." Begend-
ing: Genesis *is* Apocalypse *is* Genesis.

86.

"From the perspective of our own time, the eschatological call of Jesus initially appears as a nihilistic call to madness or to death." "Joining vision and blindness, image and judgment, hallucination and language, sleep and waking, day and night, madness is ultimately nothing, for it unites in them all that is negative. But the paradox of this *nothing* is to *manifest* itself, to explode in signs, in words, in gestures. Inextricable unity of order and disorder, of the reasonable being of things and this nothingness of madness!"

87.

"The goal cannot be the elimination of magical thinking, or madness; the goal can only be conscious magic, or conscious madness; conscious mastery of these fires. And dreaming while awake."

∘ ∘ ∘ ∘ ∘

88.

Experimentum Crucis

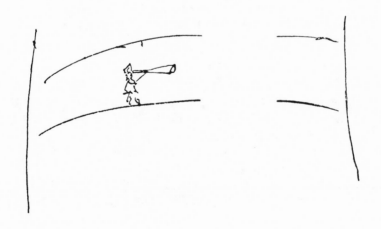

89.

Aphoristic language is gappy—full of holes. *L'espace blanc*. Silence and speech "acting together." Form *is* content.

90.

"We shall now have a closer look at the basic function of the blank as regards the guidance it exercises in the process of communication. As blanks mark the suspension of connectability between textual segments, they simultaneously form a condition for the connection to be established. By definition, however, they can clearly have no determinate content of their own. How, then, is one to describe them? As an empty space they are nothing in themselves, and yet as a 'nothing' they are a vital propellant for initiating communication." "Whenever the reader bridges the gaps, communication begins."

91.

Aphorisms form a workbook that is a workspace in which all authorship is joint authorship. "Every text, being itself the intertext of another text, belongs to the intertextual, which must not be confused with the text's origins: to search for the 'sources of' and 'influence upon' a work is to satisfy the myth of filiation. The quotations from which a text is constructed are anonymous, irrecoverable, and yet *already read*: they are quotations without quotation marks. . . . Thus . . . the text might well take as its motto the words of the man possessed by devils: 'My name is legion, for we are many.'"

92.

"The Text is plural. This does not mean just that it has several meanings, but rather that it achieves plurality of meaning, an *irreducible* plurality. The Text is not the coexistence of meanings but passage, traversal [*Metaphora*]; thus it answers not to an interpretation, liberal though it may be, but to an explosion, a dissemination. The Text's plurality does not depend on the ambiguity of its contents, but rather on what could be called the *stereographic plurality* of the signifiers that weave it. . . ."

93.

Writing is tracing, interweaving which is fabrication. The fabric of the text, however, always has loose ends. Ever unfinished, the text is a "permanent metamorphosis" which transforms reader into author and author into reader.

94.

Aphoristic writing clears a space for Alios to Inter.

o o o o o

95.

"Few are experienced enough in the
difference between an object of
scholarship and a matter of thought."

o o o o o

WORKS CONSULTED

Altizer, Thomas J. J.
1967   *The New Apocalypse: The Radical Christian Vision of
                William Blake*. East Lansing: Michigan State University Press.
1977   *The Self-Embodiment of God*. New York: Harper & Row.
1979   *The Descent Into Hell: A Study of the Radical Reversal of
                the Christian Consciousness*. New York: Seabury Press.

Barb, A. A.
1957   "Abraxas-studien." *Hommages à Waldemar Deonna*. Bruxelles.

Barfield, Owen
1957   *Saving the Appearances: A Study in Idolatry*. London: Faber
                and Faber.

Barthes, Roland
1979   "From Work to Text." *Textual Strategies: Perspectives in
                Post-Structuralist Criticism*. Ed. J. V. Harari. Ithaca: Cornell
                University Press.

Blake, William
1974   *The Illuminated Blake*. Ed. D. V. Erdman. New York:
                Doubleday.

Brown, Norman O.
  1968   *Love's Body*. New York: Random House.

Culler, Jonathan
  1975   *Structuralist Poetics: Structuralism, Linguistics and the Study
                    of Literature*. Ithaca: Cornell University Press.
  1976   *Ferdinand de Saussure*. New York: Penguin.

Derrida, Jacques
  1973   *Speech and Phenomena and Other Essays on Husserl's
                    Theory of Signs*. Trans. D. B. Allison. Evanston: Northwestern
                    University Press.
  1976   *Of Grammatology*. Trans. G. C. Spivak. Baltimore: Johns
                    Hopkins University Press.
  1978   *Writing and Difference*. Trans. A. Bass. Chicago: University of
                    Chicago Press.
  1979   "The Supplement of Copula: Philosophy *before* Linguistics."
                    *Textual Strategies: Perspectives in Post-Structuralist Criti-
                    cism*. Ed. J. V. Harari. Ithaca: Cornell University Press.

Foucault, Michel
  1975   *Madness and Civilization: A History of Insanity in the Age
                    of Reason*. Trans. R. Howard. New York: Random House.

Funk, Robert W.
  1966   *Language, Hermeneutic, and Word of God*. New York:
                    Harper & Row.
  1975   *Jesus as Precursor*. Missoula: Scholars Press.

Hegel, G. W. F.
  1968   *Lectures on the Philosophy of Religion*. Trans. E. B. Speirs
                    and J. B. Sanderson. New York: Humanities Press.
  1968   *Hegel's Science of Logic*. Trans. A. V. Miller. New York:
                    Humanities Press.
  1977   *Phenomenology of Spirit*. Trans. A. V. Miller. New York:
                    Oxford University Press.

Hart, Ray L.
  1968   *Unfinished Man and the Imagination: Toward an Ontology
                    and a Rhetoric of Revelation*. New York: Herder and Herder.

Heidegger, Martin
  1966   *Discourse on Thinking*. Trans. J. M. Anderson and E. H.
                    Freund. New York: Harper & Row.
  1971   *On the Way to Language*. Trans. P. Hertz. New York: Harper
                    & Row.
  1971   *Poetry, Language, Thought*. Trans. A. Hofstader. New York:
                    Harper & Row.
  1973   *The End of Philosophy*. Trans. J. Stambaugh. New York:
                    Harper & Row.

Hesse, Hermann
1970   *Demian: The Story of Emil Sinclair's Youth.* Trans. M. Roloff
                and M. Lebeck. New York: Bantam Books.

Iser, Wolfgang
1978   *The Act of Reading: A Theory of Aesthetic Response.*
                Baltimore: Johns Hopkins University Press.

Kazantzakis, Nikos
1965   *The Last Temptation of Christ.* Trans. P. A. Bien. New York:
                Bantam Books.

Kierkegaard, Søren
1970   *The Sickness Unto Death.* Trans. W. Lowrie. Princeton:
                Princeton University Press.

Laing, R. D.
1970   *Knots.* New York: Random House.

Merleau-Ponty, Maurice
1964   *Sense and Non-Sense.* Trans. H. L. Dreyfus and P. A.
                Dreyfus. Evanston: Northwestern University Press.
1964   *Signs.* Trans. R. C. McCleary. Evanston: Northwestern
                University Press.
1968   *The Visible and the Invisible.* Trans. A. Lingis. Evanston:
                Northwestern University Press.

Miller, J. Hillis
1979   "The Critic as Host." *Deconstruction and Criticism.* New
                York: Seabury.

Nietzsche, Friedrick
1910 ff.   *Complete Works.* Ed. O. Levy. London: Allen and Unwin.

Percy, Walker
1961   *The Moviegoer.* New York: Knopf.

Raschke, Carl A.
1979   *The Alchemy of the Word: Language and the End of Theolo-
                gy.* Missoula: Scholars Press.

Ricoeur, Paul
1970   *Freud and Philosophy: An Essay on Interpretation.* Trans. D.
                Savage. New Haven: Yale University Press.
1976   *Interpretation Theory: Discourse and the Surplus of Mean-
                ing.* Fort Worth: Texas Christian University Press.
1978   "The Metaphorical Process as Cognition, Imagination, and
                Feeling." *Critical Inquiry* 5/1:143–59.

Rosen, Stanley
1969   *Nihilism: A Philosophical Essay.* New Haven: Yale University
                Press.

Stevens, Wallace
1951   *The Necessary Angel: Essays on Reality and the Imagination.*
                New York: Knopf.

1957   *Opus Posthumous.* Ed. S. F. Morse. New York: Knopf.
1972   *The Collected Poems of Wallace Stevens.* New York: Knopf.

Smith, Morton
1978   *Jesus the Magician.* New York: Harper & Row.

Taylor, Mark C.
1978   "Toward an Ontology of Relativism." *Journal of the American
                Academy of Religion* 46/1:41–61.
1980   "Interpreting Interpretation." *Unfinished: Essays in Honor of
                Ray L. Hart.* Ed. M. C. Taylor. Chico: Scholars Press.
1980   *Journeys to Selfhood: Hegel and Kierkegaard.* Berkeley: Uni-
                versity of California Press.

Turbayne, Colin
1970   *The Myth of Metaphor.* Columbia: University of South
                Carolina Press.

Turner, Victor
1969   *The Ritual Process: Structure and Anti-Structure.* Chicago:
                Aldine Publishing Co.

The Image of the Beast, or Theology and the Thought of Difference

Carl A. Raschke

And I saw a beast rising out of the sea, with ten horns and seven heads, with ten diadems upon its horns and a blasphemous name upon its heads. And the beast that I saw was like a leopard, its feet were like a bear's, and its mouth was like a lion's mouth. And to it the dragon gave his power and his throne and great authority. One of its heads seemed to have a mortal wound, but its mortal wound was healed, and the whole earth followed the beast with wonder. Men worshiped the dragon, for he had given his authority to the beast, and they worshiped the beast, saying, "Who is like the beast, and who can fight against it?"

And the beast was given a mouth uttering haughty and blasphemous words, and it was allowed to exercise authority for forty-two months; it opened its mouth to utter blasphemies against God, blaspheming his name and his dwelling, that is, those who dwell in heaven. Also it was allowed to make war on the saints and to conquer them. And authority was given it over every tribe and people and tongue and nation, and all who dwell on earth will worship it, every one whose name has not been written before the foundation of the world in the book of life of the Lamb that was slain. If any one has an ear, let him hear:

> If any one is to be taken captive,
> to captivity he goes;
> if any one slays with the sword,
> with the sword must he be slain.

Here is a call for the endurance and faith of the saints.

Then I saw another beast which rose out of the earth; it had two horns like a lamb and it spoke like a dragon. It exercises all the authority of the first beast in its presence, and makes the earth and its inhabitants worship the first beast, whose mortal wound was healed. It works great signs, even making fire come down from heaven to earth in the sight of men; and by the signs which it is allowed to work in the presence of the beast, it deceives those who dwell on earth, bidding them make an image for the beast which was wounded by the sword and yet lived; and it was allowed to give breath to the image of the beast so that the image of the beast should even speak, and to cause those who would not worship the image of the beast to be slain. Also it causes all, both small and great, both rich and poor, both free and slave, to be marked on the right hand or the forehead, so that no one can buy or sell unless he has the

mark, that is, the name of the beast or the number of its name. This calls for
wisdom: let him who has understanding reckon the number of the beast, for it
is a human number, its number is six hundred and sixty-six. (Rev. 13 [RSV])

1.

The "number" of the beast (666) is a "human number." It is a synthetic
number. Six is the number of the penultimate, of the finite trenching upon
the infinite. Six signifies the day on which man was crafted in God's "image"
and "after his likeness" (Gen. 1:26). The beast consists in a treble multiplica-
tion of the inborn powers of man. Whereas six belongs to the gematria of
divine "likeness," three betokens the invigoration of that representation.
Three is the cipher for creation. On the third day God brought into being
the earth, its verdancy, its capacity for fecundity (Gen. 1:9–13). The beast is
nought but God's "image" and "likeness" imbued with primal creative
potency or "breath." ". . . And it was allowed to give breath to the image of
the beast so that the image of the beast should even speak . . ." (Rev. 13:15).

Speech, *logos*, articulate discourse—that is what constitutes the specific
difference within the genus "animal" which yields "humanity." Language is
only possible when the human aptitude for imaging, for diachronous repli-
cation, is animated by divine breath, by the *ruach* or spirit that comprises
the power not only to register impressions from, but to transfigure, the
world. Adam's acquisition of the breath, his metamorphosis from dust into a
"living being" or *nephesh* (Gen. 2:7), imparted to him the facility for
"naming." In this connection the "beast" (*to therion*) stands for something
much greater and more awesome than man's "animal" nature and origins. It
possesses all the traits and virtues of the antelapsarian Adam, of the still
unitary "image." Furthermore, these virtues are not only preserved, but
augmented in a triplex fashion by God's creative energy. Thus the beast is
not a counterforce to, but the perfection of, creation. Like life itself, it arises
out of the "sea" and out of the "earth." It is stamped with the "image" of
living divinity. Yet its "authority" (*exousia*) is not from God, but from the
"dragon." It has the form of the Christ, although in substance it is the anti-
Christ. It speaks what sounds most essential and holy, but its words are
exposed as "blasphemous."

The image of the beast is an apocalyptic image: it is an image that
coincides with the eschatological turnabout, with history's grand reversal,
with Nietzsche's "transvaluation of values." In the grand reversal the constel-
lations of good and evil, truth and semblance, wisdom and folly, sanity and
madness, are capsized and set on end. What hitherto was apprehended
proleptically as God's presence is disclosed at the moment of *apocalypsis*
(literally, "unveiling" or "manifesting") as God's absence. What was
cherished as a divine showing is seen as a mere "likeness." The first becomes
last, the savior the adversary, the church the "synagogue of Satan." The

beast is revelation of the minute, yet infinite difference between man and God, between representation and truth as *alētheia* ("unconcealedness"). The beast is an artifact not of man's instinctual promptings, but of his quest for rational certitude and moral perfection (cf. Goya's adage: "the dream of reason breeds monsters"). The image of the beast is deciphered as the self-reflection, as the ghost in the mirror, of Western man's metaphysical gaze. The image does not materialize within the history of Western religious thought, because it has previously remained *unthought*. The shock of recognition attendant upon the discernment of the image does not occur within the career of theology, but transpires at the *end of theology*./1/

2.

Infinite alterity as death cannot be reconciled with infinite alterity as positivity and presence (God). Metaphysical transcendence cannot be at once transcendence towards the other as Death and transcendence towards the other as God. Unless God means Death, which after all has never been *exluded* by the entirety of the classical philosophy within which we understand God both as Life and as the Truth of Infinity, of positive Presence. But what does this *exclusion* mean if not the exclusion of every particular *determination*? And that God is *nothing* (determined), is not life, because he is *everything*? and therefore is at once All and Nothing, Life and Death. Which means that God is or appears, *is named*, within the difference between All and Nothing, Life and Death. Within difference, and at bottom as Difference itself. This difference is what is called History. God is inscribed in it. (Derrida:115–16)

To name God in finality and fullness, however, is to rouse the beast. The archaeological recovery of the divine inscription upon the tablets of history must inevitably bestir the serpent guarding them. That is because the naming of God compasses the knowledge of difference; it entails a discrimination between truth and semblance, between visage and likeness. This likeness, moreover, is the re-presentation, the spurious identity, that clouds the difference between presence and absence, between life and death, between Yahweh and Satan, between vision and false prophecy. This likeness persists under the guise of truth throughout history. It gives impetus to history itself, although it remains hidden until the close of the age. When likeness is at least posed as difference, however, God must be made manifest, not as logical identity-in-difference, but as the unthought presence that bodies forth *from within difference*. With the revelation of an erstwhile likeness now as difference, the likeness itself is no longer holiness, but the eschatological *lie*.

3.

The recognition of the difference between God's essence and likeness must inaugurate the worship of the beast, which constitutes the supreme form of idolatry. An idol is but a depotentiated deity. In German an "idol" is an *Abgott*, a god who has "fallen away" or been subtracted from the perfection of the Godhead. Idolatry is likeness mistaken for correspondence. It is this misperception, the denial of difference, that spawns the beast. For the "image" (*eikon*) of the beast, as an eidetic representation, is distinguishable at first from the form of God. This neglect to draw a distinction derives from the passion for identity combined with the recoil from difference. The shortcoming is a human one, as is the number of the beast.

4.

The ocular experience of depth—stereoscopic vision—depends on the apprehension of difference. The right eye picks up the same impressions as the left eye although from a slightly different angle. The angular discrepancy supplies a modicum of information that comes to be extrapolated as a three-dimensional body. Single-pointed vision is not able to make this discrimination and thus falters in mapping the full set of spatial coordinates. Only with a slight, but telling divergence of two lines of sight (i.e., with the inkling of difference) can stenoscopic sight be surpassed and multiple dimensionality brought into focus. Just as integral calculus presupposes differential operations, so the achievement of cognitive synthesis demands nuance and distinction.

According to Gregory Bateson, who has surveyed from both a cybernetic and psychological standpoint this "method of double comparison, any two patterns may, if appropriately combined, generate a third" (1979:89). The converse of double comparison, however, is false assimilation. False assimilation involves an inattention to difference for the sake of abstract unity. It is a procrustean fusion of discrepant energies or patterns. Whereas double comparison is necessary to the envisioning of the new Jerusalem, false assimilation results in the shotgun marriage of heaven and hell. It is the dowry of the beast.

5.

Let us consider, for example, Hegel's discussion of the double "play of forces" in the *Phenomenology of Spirit*, in which the sensible and the supersensible, "inner" and "outer," finite and infinite, are reconciled only through the profession of difference. The disclosure of difference points up a "*difference* which is no difference, or only a difference of what is *self-same*, and its essence is unity" (1977:99). But the self-reflection movement from bare identity through difference to "identity-in-difference" is more than the simple elaboration of opposites. In the transitional phase the opposites themselves must be exposed as reciprocal, interchangeable, and in certain respects indistinguishable. The double play of forces, which contains within it "the principle of change and alteration," must obey "the law of the inverted world." "According, then, to the law of this inverted world, what is *like* in the first world is equally *unlike to itself*, or it becomes *like* itself. Expressed in determinate moments, this means that what in the law of the first world is sweet, in this inverted in-itself is sour, what in the former is black is, in the other, white" (1977:97). Yet this difference between "worlds" is, in actuality, an "inner difference," a dynamic duplicity within the thing as it becomes manifest. It is equivalent to "a repulsion of the self-same, as self-same, from itself, and likeness of the unlike as unlike" (1977:99). Life, or Spirit, for Hegel, is self-division aimed toward self-integration. Likeness must be divulged as unlikeness to release the harmonious tension of thing's living essence. The dead God must be changed into Satan in order to be reborn as living divinity. The image of the beast is not disconnected from the idea of God; it is only the inverted impression of the divine with the theological *camera obscura*.

6.

Just as "force" in Hegel's phenomenology splits not so much "worlds" as the husk of entities from their activated kernels, so the "divine" winnows "God" from "man." The meaning of "incarnation," for Hegel, was that the "essence" of man *qua* Spirit becomes self-reflective; the "inverted" world of the unhappy consciousness is finally rejoined with itself. God in his alterity is shown to be the *dynamis*, the immanent divine power, sequestered like nuclear energy within the human.

The liberation of the energy that is God from the "matter" that is man is foreshadowed in Nietzsche's notion of the *Übermensch* ("overman"). Zarathustra proclaims: "Behold, I am a herald of the lightning and a heavy drop from the cloud; but this lightning is called *overman*" (1954:128). Whence the lightning? It is the thunderbolt that crackles from the nimbus of what is essentially human. The thunderbolt is the materialization of the infinite "danger" that was implicit in man's own self-scrutiny. For self-scrutiny unveils the infinite "above and below," the awesome potential that is "man." What is man? Zarathustra speaks: "A dangerous across, a dangerous on-the-way, a dangerous looking back, a dangerous shuddering and stopping" (1954:126). For "man is a rope, tied between beast and overman—a rope over an abyss" (126). The fall of man, the tight-rope walker, occurs east of Eden; it takes place when man can no longer navigate the slender wire, when he is poised to hurtle toward the "beyond" of overman. If overman is the lightning explosion, then the beast is the fallout. The explosion parts the divine from its likeness; that is the infinite danger. The divine likeness, of course, is the beast's image.

7.

If overman is the revelation of the indwelling presence, the beast is the showing of the sacral re-presentation which has masqueraded throughout the Christian era as the highest "God." The beast may also be stamped "desire," the binding of free energy, the homing of the "will" on a calculable object, the cathexis of instinctual drives toward a discrete psychic formation (Freud). The re-presentation of divine presence, which has justified and sustained the Christian theological tradition since the Apologists, has not defined God so much as it has tethered the beast. "Re-presentative thinking" (Heidegger) rather than Christianity, as Nietzsche believed, is the two-thousand-year legacy for which the promissory note has at long last fallen due.

According to Michael Foucault,

> the obscure but stubborn spirit of a people who talk, the violence and the endless effort of life, the hidden energy of needs, were all to escape from the mode of being of representation. And representation itself was to be paralleled, limited, circumscribed, mocked perhaps, but in any case regulated from the outside, by the enormous thrust of freedom, a desire, or a will, posited as the metaphysical converse of consciousness. Something like a will or a force was to arise in the modern experience—constituting it perhaps, but in any case indicating that the Classical age was now over, and with it the reign of representative discourse, the dynasty of a representation signifying itself and giving voice in the sequence of its words to the order that lay dormant within things. (1970:209)

Re-presentative discourse is governed by the metaphysics of likeness; it establishes what Derrida has termed "the age of the sign," where meaning is no longer presence, but *reference.* Such a metaphysics merely encloses for time the violence of desire. Desire erupts when it can no longer enframe the divine. It becomes a form of arcane voyeurism.

8.

Zarathustra's "dancing song": ". . . the devil is the spirit of gravity" (Nietzsche:219).

Re-presentative thinking—metaphysics, theology—is the habitation of the devil in Nietzsche's sense. Modern thought has been possessed with the devil since Descartes. The demon of the *Meditations,* who beguiled Descartes with his intimations of uncertainty, proves to have been the divine in disguise. By the same token, Descartes's God is the *persona* of the devil. For the devil forces all that is vital, fluid, mobile, sensible into a moribund re-presentation, an *eidos,* a geometric character, into the Cartesian *quod clare et distincte.* The devil's gravity shrinks truth to a patent certainty. "I always lived attached," Descartes wrote in his *Discourse Concerning*

Method, "to the resolve I had taken to suppose no other principle except that which I just used to demonstrate the existence of God and the soul, and to accept nothing as true that did not seem to me clear and more certain than the demonstrations of the geometers had formerly seemed" (1977:141). Must we consider Descartes's "attachment" and "resolve" an act of piety, or a demonic obsession? Theology traffics with the devil, even if it has exchanged Descartes's *cogito* for the contemporary *experior*.

9.

Any solution to the question of difference within the ambit of philosophical hermeneutics must be negotiated along with the controversy between Heidegger and Hegel. Heidegger remarks:

> For Hegel, the conversation with the earlier history of philosophy has the character of *Aufhebung*, that is, of the mediating concept in the sense of an absolute foundation.
>
> For us, the character of the conversation with the history of thinking is no longer *Aufhebung* (elevation), but the step back [*der Schritt zurück*].
>
> Elevation leads to the heightening and gathering area of truth posited as absolute, truth in the sense of the completely developed certainty of self-knowing knowledge.
>
> The step back points to the realm which until now has been skipped over, and from which the essence of truth becomes first of all worthy of thought. (1969:49)

For Hegel, "difference" implies *dissemblance*, the diremption of essence and appearance in order that thought can be objectified to itself (1977:377). This self-objectification, or self-distancing (*Entäusserung*), the transition from the in-itself (*an sich*) to the for-itself (*für sich*), is necessary so that "reason" can attain to its own self-certainty. Self-certainty comes with the "elevation" of previously antithetical contents of thinking into the unity Hegel characterizes as "science." Difference passes over into the self-reflective instant of speculative identity. The discordant phases of the intellectual tradition are comprehended in both their mutuality and tension. The history of philosophy is transposed into the philosophy of history.

For Heidegger, "difference" is no longer a tension or a dissemblance, but a horizon beyond which the re-presentative, self-mirroring activity of philosophical reasoning is barred. Difference connotes not a new thought of immanence, but an intimation of transcendence (Derrida's "infinite alterity" = Heidegger's "ontological difference"). Heidegger's thought of difference is not the thought, as it remains for Hegel, of identity-in-difference, but of difference *as* difference, the ontological difference between Being and beings, between presence and re-presentation. For Heidegger, the "Sameness" of thinking and Being is not disclosed as a synthetic unity among the monents of *dianoia*, but the "belonging together" (*Zugehörigkeit*) of man and Being. *Zugehörigkeit* is etymologically linked with *zuhören* ("to listen to" or "attend to"). Man opens himself to the presencing of Being by attending or responding to what "calls" him from beyond the ontological horizon. For "man's distinctive feature lies in this, that he, as the being who thinks, is open to Being, face to face with Being; thus man remains referred to Being and so answers to it. Man *is* essentially this relationship of responding to Being, and he is only this" (1969:30).

Hence, according to Heidegger, to think the difference *as* difference is to think "back" to the origin, to the essential, *intimate* relationship between man and Being that has been eclipsed by the history of metaphysical or "objectifying" reasoning. To think difference in this fashion is to think through the *re-presentative* or iconic aspects of philosophical ideas and to recover the primordial context in which Being shows itself. Heidegger's hermeneutics of the Western tradition leads back to the indication of originary presence, to *theos* or "shining divinity," which remains antecedent to all re-presentation. Heidegger's quarrel with Hegel, founded on the presumption that in the dialectical ingathering of representations (*Vorstellungen*) it is not originary presence that is thought anew, but the assimilation of Being to self-reflection, the apotheosis of the Cartesian *ego cogito* as the subjective mirror play of all elements of knowledge./2/ Hegel's speculative system, therefore, marks the climax of the career of Western metaphysics, and it can only precede or prefigure the Heideggerian project of "overcoming" re-presentative thinking.

Nonetheless, it must be asked whether Heidegger has not hewn a straw man out of Hegel and whether the latter has not grappled with the thought of difference on a much more innovative, profound plane than that with which he has been credited. Indeed, it may well be the case that the Hegelian movement of *Aufhebung* amounts to something far more significant than the dialectical nuptials of re-presentational elements, as Heidegger claims. Moreover, Heidegger's principal venture of hermeneutical thinking, namely, the "step back" from speculative identity to ontological difference, from the coherence of theological and metaphysical statements to the "veiled" presencing of the divine, may not be all that far removed from Hegel's own tacit agenda. For the aim of dialectic, Hegel suggests, is also to "think through" the ostensible meanings of all re-presentations or *Vorstellungen* so as to lay bare their concealed semantic potentials. Their semantic potentials are generated by the tension of difference between immanence and transcendence, between the latent and manifest. It can be argued as well that even Hegel's "self-knowing Spirit," which actualizes itself by bridging the difference between inner and outer, does not ultimately betray the "subjecticity" of modern metaphysics, as Heidegger insists, but sparks a disclosure of divine presence in a guise that serves as an unprecedented cue for "thinking the unthought." The basis for such an inference concerning Hegel's intentions is not evident in either the *Phenomenology* or even in the *Logic*. On the contrary, it is located in the third volume of *Lectures on the Philosophy of Religion*. Here Hegel adopts the same hermeneutical point of departure as do Nietzsche and Heidegger, who have all charted the philosophical terrain of the post-metaphysical epoch. Like his predecessors, Hegel registers the "end" of both theology and metaphysics through recognition of the "not" of Being itself, in a word, through the announcement of the death of God.

By Hegel's account the death of God, the divine *kenosis* or "emptying" of the infinite into concrete life, is the pivot of the history of consciousness. The death of God bespeaks the *crucial* transit, the dialectical shift of direction, within the "history of God." For the history of God turns upon the elevation of the "finite" within the sphere of the infinite; and this turning or "reversal," which for Hegel counts as the revelation of God not as *totaliter aliter* but as indwelling Spirit, can only arise at the moment of absolute negation, with the divine death, which Hegel terms *die Lücke des Lebens* ("the chasm of life"). "*God has died, God is dead*: this is the most frightful of all thought, that everything eternal and true does not exist, that negation itself is found in God. The deepest anguish, the feeling of something completely irretrievable, the abandoning of everything that is elevated, are bound up with this thought" (1979:212).

The death of God is the event of divine self-alienation, of the Spirit pouring into all "flesh," of infinity steeping itself within the finite. But this instance of self-negation is akin to the rest point in the arc of a pendulum. "The process does not come to a halt at this point; rather, a reversal takes place: God . . . maintains himself in this process, and the latter is only the death of death. God rises again to life, and thus things are reversed" (212). The "reversal" accompanies the epiphany of "difference" within the divine nature itself. For God's death means that there is no longer any cleavage between finite and infinite, between human and divine. Finite and infinite coinhere within the divine essence, and both thereby imbue the character and destiny of man. The stress between the antipodes in both God and man defines the unity and self-unfolding tendencies of Spirit. And the "rising" of God, whereupon difference is transcended not as logical identity but as the reunion of Spirit with itself, becomes the chief metaphor for the divine movement within history.

Yet God's ascension, which is at the same time man's resurrection, has until now not been unveiled in its fullness of presence (*parousia*). Instead of having been manifested as divine presence, the death and regeneration of God has persisted for centuries only in historical memory as a re-presentation, as an image. The divine presencing "is given only in an individual, and it is not capable of being inherited or renewed. This cannot happen because a sensible appearance such as this is by its very nature momentary and must be spiritualized; it is essentially something that *has been*, and it will be raised up into the domain of representation" (214). Since the dawn of the Christian era the re-presentation of God's death and transfiguration has stalked the theological mind. But the re-presentation is not yet *parousia*, is not yet the self-revelation of Spirit. For Hegel, religion is raised to the status of philosophy when the re-presentation (*Vorstellungen*) is "thought" in its implicit and essential meaning, as *Gedanken*. God's dying on the Cross, preserved throughout history as a mnemonic figuration, is finally thought hermeneutically as the death of God *within history*. The figuration is shown in the conclusion of things to be not divine presence, but absence. Although philosophy has thought the death of God, as disclosure of *difference* within God, it has still not comprehended the divine "rising." It has failed to think beyond absence to "total presence" (Altizer), to *parousia*; it has not thought through to the Spirit that comes to presence only through the transcendence of difference. Such presence is what Hegel implies by his notion of identity-in-difference, which is analogous to Nietzsche's "overman." In theological parlance, we might say it is not the singular event of divine instantiation, but *permanent incarnation* which has previously been unthought. When the re-presentation of incarnation is thought in its difference from total presence, then the "reversal" has fructified historically. The historical re-presentation of Christ, the shadow of the Cross, is held up to view as anti-Christ. Traditional Christian theology is left holding the reins of the beast.

10.

We are at the end of the "Roman" epoch in Western culture. The "Roman" period should be limned less in terms of the overt influence of classic style or Latin jurisprudence than with respect to the perdurance of "foundationalist" habits of thinking. Hannah Arendt has argued that the whole of the ancient Roman *Weltbild* gravitated toward the idea that civilization and its imperial prerogatives were secured in the "founding" of the *civitas aeterna*./3/ The Roman mind set that construed intellectual inquiry as a species of *traditio* and culture as a cumulative "building upon foundations" came to inhabit the assumptions and method of Christian theology for centuries following Alaric the Goth's rampages. When Luther contravened the supreme authority of the Pope in matters ecclesiastical, he still did not throw off the invisible halter of Roman foundationalism within the preserve of faith. Protestantism, as many historians have intoned, merely redescribed the bulwarks of belief. For "Church" Luther substituted the "word of God," for Papal bulls the teachings of Christ and Paul. It was up to Enlightenment rationalism, which took its commission from the Renaissance rather than the Reformation, from classicism instead of primitive Christianity, to shed all vestiges of religious absolutism and to ply its own version of "foundationalist" epistemology on the basis of the "self-evident" truths of science and reason.

The foundationalist attitude toward the world, as Richard Rorty in a most timely book on the trials of contemporary philosophy has shown us, is derived from the metaphysical premise that all knowledge can be made "commensurate" with (i.e., occasioned to "mirror") certain "privileged representations" (1979:170). These "representations" are the apodictic footing on which judgment of truth and falsity, sense and nonsense, can be soundly made. Just as Christian theology has had the Bible and patristic precedents to construct its own framework of commensurable representations, so modern philosophy has appealed to the certainty of mathematical relations (rationalism), secondary qualities (empiricism), transcendental concepts (Kantianism), protocol statements (positivism), or "depth grammar" (linguistic analysis). For generations these re-presentations were taken as simulacra or "pictures" of reality, when it is now becoming apparent, even to philosophers who have tried longer than any discipline to seize the foundationalist's will-o-the-wisp, that they are nothing more than "maps" susceptible to revision, if the terrain is scouted differently.

The transition from re-presentation to mapping coincides, according to Rorty, with the change from foundationalism to "holism," from epistemology to hermeneutics, from "method" to "interpretation," from "confrontation" to "conversation." Rorty's docket for philosophy is similar to Foucault's program for all the "human sciences." The end of re-presentative thought in every domain means, in Foucault's judgment, that we no longer speak dualistically of language and reference, or about concept and object, but about "discursive formations" that constitute "uninterrupted movement of totalizations, the return to an ever open source" (1976:39). This "ever open source" is not the same as the foundation or "beginning" in the sense of the metaphysical *arché*, the theological *revelatum*, the evangelical *vera religio*, the philosophical *a priori*. It is not beginning, but *origin*, which is not re-membered or re-presented, but consists in the ongoing and intimate e-vent ("coming forth") of presence.

The latter day "fall of Rome," or of Roman foundationalism, particularly with regard to theology, means that the re-presentations "God" and "Christ" must crumble with the inbreaking of divine presence. The "end of theology" therefore is concomitant with *parousia*. Yet Rome does not pacifically relinquish its power. It is the dragon that must parry the upending of the world's foundations. The guardian of "tradition" and the "shepherd of Christ" must mobilize against the earthquake that causes its battlements to shudder. At the close of the age the faith's defenders must become the legions of the anit-Christ. The reign of the beast lasts forty-two months, a period of convulsion and instability.

11.

Opposed to the distinction between deep 'essences' and surface 'accidents' structuralism teaches that all the accidents are to be included in an interpretation. Like Hegel's phenomenology in finding order *among* the phenomena

rather than in *noumena* behind the phenomena, like hermeneutic psychoanalysis in taking each 'accidental' slip of the tongue as a tool for interpretation, a structuralist reading of contemporary spiritual phenomena would
dismiss nothing as merely 'superficial,' merely 'accidental.' Nor need a
structuralist reading fall into some single profoundity whose power, however
secular and this-worldly in appearance, would betray in its neat clarity its
heritage as a transform of monotheism. (Ogilvy:274)

While such a structuralist hermeneutics may succeed in tracing fibers of
intelligibility covertly interwoven beneath every visible exterior, it cannot
delve to the very ganglion of noetic relations. The "information" generated
by the structuralist method, therefore, can be compared to a sham progression of knowledge, a self-enclosed nexus of re-presentations disguised as a
movement between epistemic levels, which in cybernetic parlance is known
as a "strange loop."/4/

The strange loop, as an example of hermeneutical disclosure, has the semblance of Hegel's "good infinity." It appears to have made a dialectical leap, to
have both spurred and relaxed the tension of difference. In actuality, however,
difference has never been broached, let alone transcended. A "revelation"
seems to occur, when in fact we have merely the eternal repetition of the
same. The alleged interconnectedness of things is purely self-referential and
hence cannot genuinely be counted as a hidden thematic pattern.
Structuralism is capable of "saving the appearances" only so far as it mistakes
the logical types under which empirical data can be subsumed for a deeper
unity of meaning. It cannot fathom that the very essence of thought is not a
timeless and unstreaked looking glass in which the *cogito* beholds its only
infinity of possible re-presentations, but a reserve of unthought presence.

Whereas a structuralist hermeneutics is inescapably coupled to a pluralist interpretation of phenomena and remains formally critical of all "monotheistic" explanations, a *radical* or archaeological approach seeks to uncover
the "originary" source from which all re-presentations and morphological
links radiate. From the standpoint of radical hermeneutics, the links themselves are not causal or spatio-temporal properties of events; rather, they are
phantoms in the etymological sense of the word. "Phantom" derives from
the Greek *phaino* (= "to manifest"). As phantoms they are at the same time

semiophanies ("meaning-manifestations"). A radical hermeneutics brings to light through interpretation of apparent "accidents" not a unity of thought, or a grammatical structure, but a community of symbols and thought-contents manifested within the unity of the unthought. It discloses all re-presentations as "phantoms"—as mirages from the ultimate ontological standpoint, but also as interrelated *manifestations* of what is *au fond* unmanifest.

The cognate field of inquiry for radical hermeneutics is quantum physics. According to Gary Zukav, the new "philosophy of science" builds upon the Buddhist conception of "enlightenment," which is similar to Heidegger's thinking of the unthought. Zukav contends:

> A vital aspect of the enlightened state is the experience of an all-pervading unity. 'This' and 'that' no longer are separate entities. They are different *forms* of the same thing. Everything is a *manifestation*. It is not possible to answer the question, 'Manifestation of *what?*' because the 'what' is that which is beyond words, beyond concept, beyond form, beyond even space and time. (1979:281)

This unitary interplay of reciprocal manifestations is the provenance of the so-called "acausal meanings" Carl Jung denoted by the expression "synchronicity." Surprisingly, it also has been summed up in a particular cosmological principle known as Bell's theorem. Bell's theorem implies that "the 'separate parts' of the universe are connected in an intimate and immediate way" (282). The "superluminal" and manifold interconnectedness of things, as delineated in Bell's theorem, raises the radical possibility that all logical identities, mathematical equivalences, and conceptual re-presentations are samples of "false assimilation." For the fallacy of false assimilation stems from a perceptual disorder whereby one fails to make subtle discriminations and tends to spot regularities where there are actually variances.

If Bell's theorem holds, then both the monistic and pluralist accounts of the universe are wobbly. Bell's theorem suggests an infinite diversity of entities or phenomena which are, in any event, all unified in a single "field" of interaction and unfoldment. All thought, past and present, therefore shows itself not as a system of determinations, but as an indeterminate horizon of the unthought. Yet this unthought is not the same as a "gap" in firm knowledge or a mystical *je ne sais quoi*. In some ways the very "thought" of the unthought constitutes the key to Gödel's dilemma. Gödel, the famous mathematician who demonstrated the ultimate limits of any system of inference, left us with the impression that the Absolute can be allowed only if it cannot be proven. For the Absolute is not a logical identity, but the *fons et origo* of all manifestations. It is not "God" in the idiom of theologians, but the "divine" presence which suffuses, illumines, and knits together all beings; it is the presence that cannot be re-presented, even as the *prima causa*; it is the creative plenum that winks through the space of *difference*.

Must we call this creative plenum "God"? The term conjures up a clutch of metaphysical ideas or re-presentations. Previously God has served as the prevailing *designatum* for the unmanifest. But God in the end must be seen to have been a re-presentation "split off" by metaphysical thought from the plenum. The splitting off of thought contents, like components of the psyche, can have perilous consequences. When God is split from the plenum, he is revealed to be what he is in truth—the chaos monster, the beast.

12.

In Book XII of the *Confessions* Augustine muses on the mystery of creation and the primordial ambivalence between the "formed" and the "formless."

> I find that there are two things which you have created outside the realm of time, though neither of that two is coeternal with you. One of these is so formed that, though changeable, it is, nevertheless, unchanged and is able without any intermission of contemplation, without any interval of change, perfectly to enjoy eternity and changelessness. And the other was so formless that it could not change from one form to another, whether of motion or rest, and consequently was not subject to time. (1963:292)

The "formless" corresponds to what Augustine dubs "the rolling vicissitudes of time"; it is not unlike Plato's *apeiron* ("receptacle") mentioned in the *Timaeus*. Yet, in contrast to Plato's receptacle, Augustine's "formless" stuff is energic and creative. It is no longer refractory *necessity* (*ananke*), but dynamic potentiality. Whereas in Plato's cosmogonic myth, as in most Greek philosophy, the "animating" principle is lodged in "form," for Augustine the fillip of vital existence comes from the roiling expanse of the "formless." Whereas the Greeks had expressly re-presented God as *eidos*,/5/ in opposition to *chaos*, Augustinian Christianity recognized both form and formlessness as "coeternal" possibilities within divine creation. Moreover, Augustine saw the formless not merely as the antithesis of the divine, but as the matrix of its manifestation. For the divine itself is not form, but the uncreated "light" by which all forms can be illumined or made manifest. And the formless constitutes the very power of "life" which, once illumined, becomes the presencing of the living God.

> At the beginning of the creation you said: *Let there be light, and there was light*. I think I have good reason to take these words as referring to the spiritual creation, for there was already a life of sort for you to illuminate. But just as it had no claim upon you to be of a kind capable of illumination, so, when it did exist, it had no claim actually to be illuminated. Its formless state could not please you unless it became light, and became light not simply by existing but by beholding the light shining upon it and by cleaving to it; so that it owed entirely to your grace both its life and the happiness of that life, being turned, by a change for the better, toward that which can suffer no change

> either for the better or the worse—toward you, who alone exist in simplicity,
> to whom it is not one thing to live and another to live happily. (318)

The formless is the origin of *transformation*—of mere life into "divine" life, of darkness into light, of matter into spirit, of "beast" into overman. The formless, like the resplendent light of divinity that breaks forth from it, cannot be re-presented. To re-present the divine is to compress it, bridle it, stultify it, to inhibit the vital, transformative process. To re-present it, as the history of Christian theology has done, is to swage the semblance of divine life as a bland immobility. To re-present the divine, as in all idolatry, is to kill God. That is what theology, horrified like the ancient Hellenes at the intimations of the infinite and formless and too timid to think the difference between presence and re-presentation, between truth and likeness, has done.

But this theological *eikon* that has passed for centuries by the name of God packs within itself not only the promise of creative life, but also the fury of the formless (what the Greeks described as *to deinon*, "the violent"). The "split" or "dead" re-presentation of God is made puissant; it is aswarm with destructive tendencies. In the apocalyptic inversion *the God of Christian theology is unmasked as Satan.*/6/ For Satan is the symbol for the theological nisus, for the desire to "bind" the energy of the divine, to enframe or re-present it, to besiege and conquer "heaven." In Book II of *Paradise Lost* Milton has Satan declare:

> Powers and dominions, deities of heaven,
> For since no deep within her gulf can hold
> Immortal vigor, though oppressed and fallen,
> I give not heaven for lost. From this descent
> Celestial virtues rising, will appear
> More glorious and more dread than from no fall . . .

Satan's "immortal vigor" is the chaotic agitation of life yoked to the service of a sacral re-presentation. For the Satanic restlessness constitutes the obverse side of God's imperturbability. The formless surges within the confines of theological form. The beast slumbers unnoticed within the ramparts of the heavenly city, still to be awakened by the trumpets of the Last Judgment.

After God dies, the beast must be unleashed "for a little while," only to be conquered in the end by the divine *logos* that is "unnamed" and beyond re-presentation (Rev.19:12), in other words, by the boundless energy of creation.

13.

In the past, theology has busied itself with thinking the unity of God. To attain this unity it had to enclose God as an ultimate re-presentation. First it re-presented God as Creator or paternal progenitor, then as the Crucified

One, or as Son. Each re-presentation of unity, however, "split" God off from the divine plenitude and damped the tension of difference. For example, the unity of God as Creator gives rise to the thought of difference between the infinite and finite. The unity of God as Son reduces the strain between infinity and finitude, yet lays bare the difference between initiation and completion, between incarnation and *eschaton*, between the human and the posthuman. For the divine is the term of completion, the transcendence of the difference between re-presentation and presence, between Christ and the Christification of life, between God and "overman." The difference is transcended at Zarathustra's "great noon," where apocalypse becomes the resurrection of God. *"Dead are all gods: now we want the overman to live"* (Nietzsche:191). But this transcendence of difference can only happen when the difference itself is thought through to its unthought depth. Just as the thinking of Bell's theorem, according to Zukav, leads to the "end of science," so the thinking of unthought divinity eventuates in the "end of theology." Apocalypse is both the thought, and the transcendence of the thought, of *difference*. It is an ending that is in the same moment a new beginning. The ending comes with theology's own self-revelation, once it beholds its own re-presentations in a mirror. In the mirror it glimpses not the face of God, but the image of the beast. It detects not faith, but desire, not divine majesty, but man's will to power. Yet beyond this thought is not God's death, which has already been thought through, but the immanent rebirth of living divinity, the lightning that flashes from out of the tenebrous abyss that is both the abode of the beast and the truth behind the reflection in the crystal pool into which man peers.

NOTES

/1/   For an explanation of what is implied in the phrase "end" of theology, see Raschke.

/2/   See Heidegger (1973:29).

/3/   See the essay "What is Authority?" in Arendt:91–142.

/4/   For an excellent discussion of cybernetics and the significance of the "strange loop" in logic and art, see Hofstadter.

/5/   See Bennett.

/6/   This point is incisively made by Altizer in his recent book.

WORKS CONSULTED

Altizer, Thomas J. J.
1980   *Total Presence.* New York: Seabury Press.

Augustine of Hippo
1963   *Confessions.* Trans. Rex Warner. New York: New American Library.

Arendt, Hannah
1961   *Between Past and Future.* New York: Viking Press.

Bateson, Gregory
1979   *Mind and Nature.* New York: E. P. Dutton.

Bennett, Curtis
1976   *God as Form.* Albany: State Uiversity of New York Press.

Derrida, Jacques
1978   *Writing and Difference.* Trans. Alan Bass. Chicago: University of Chicago Press.

Descartes, Rene
1977   *Essential Writings.* Trans. John Blow. New York: Harper & Row.

Foucault, Michael
1976   *The Archaeology of Knowledge.* Trans. A. M. Sheridan Smith. New York: Harper & Row.
1978   *The Order of Things.* New York: Pantheon Books.

Hegel, G. W. F.
1977   *The Phenomenology of Spirit.* Trans. A. V. Miller. Oxford: Oxford University Press.
1979   *The Christian Religion.* Trans. Peter Hodgson. Missoula, MT: Scholars Press.

Heidegger, Martin
1969   *Identity and Difference.* Trans. Joan Stambaugh. New York: Harper & Row.
1973   *The End of Philosophy.* Trans. Joan Stambaugh. New York: Harper & Row.

Hofstadter, Douglas
1979   *Gödel, Escher, Bach.* New York: Basic Books.

Ogilvy, James
1979   *Many-Dimensional Man.* New York: Harper & Row.

Nietzsche, Friedrich
1954   *The Portable Nietzsche.* Trans. Walter Kaufman. New York: The Viking Press.

Raschke, Carl A.
1979   *The Alchemy of the Word.* Missoula, MT: Scholars Press.

Rorty, Richard
    1979   *Philosophy and the Mirror of Nature.* Princeton, NJ: Princeton University Press.
Zukav, Gary
    1979   *The Dancing Wu-Li Masters.* New York: William Morrow.

NOTES ON CONTRIBUTORS

DAVID B. BURRELL, C.S.C., Professor of Philosophy and Theology at the University of Notre Dame, has served as Chair of the Department of Theology at that institution from 1971–80, and Rector of the Ecumenical Institute for Theological Research (Tantur) in Jerusalem from 1980–81. Holding a B.A. from Notre Dame, he pursued studies for the priesthood in Rome (S.T.L., Gregorianum, 1960) and doctoral studies in Philosophy at Yale (Ph.D., 1965). Author of *Analogy and Philosophical Language, Exercises in Religious Understanding*, and *Aquinas: God and Action*, he is presently engaged in exploring the Islamic and Jewish influences on the classical Christian formulations of the doctrine of God.

DAVID R. CROWNFIELD is Professor of Religion and Philosophy at the University of Northern Iowa. He studied at Harvard and Yale, and holds the Ph.D. in Systematic Theology from Harvard. He has published a number of articles on topics dealing with consciousness, culture, and religion in the *Journal of the American Academy of Religion* and in the *North American Review*.

ROBERT O. JOHANN is Professor of Philosophy at Fordham University. He received his Ph.D. from Louvaine University and his S.T.L. from Woodstock College. He is author of *The Meaning of Love* (1955), *The Pragmatic Meaning of God*, and *Building the Human* (1968), and he has edited the volume *Freedom and Value* (1976). He has published articles in such journals as the *Review of Metaphysics* and *International Philosophical Quarterly*.

CARL A. RASCHKE is Associate Professor of Religious Studies at the University of Denver and holds his Ph.D. from Harvard University. He is currently editor of the AAR Academy Series. He is author of *Moral Action, God, and History in the Thought of Immanuel Kant* (1975); *Religion and the Human Image* (co-author 1977); *The Bursting of New Wineskins* (1978); *The Alchemy of the Word* (1979); *The Interruption of Eternity* (1980). He has also published articles in *Harvard Theological Review, Philosophy Today*, and *Journal of the American Academy of Religion*.

PETER SLATER is Professor of Religion at Carleton University in Ottawa, Canada, and Co-Chairperson of the Cross-Cultural Philosophy of Religions Group of the American Academy of Religion. He is author of *The Dynamics of Religion* (1978) and editor with others of *Traditions in Contact and Change* (1981). He received his Ph.D. from Harvard with distinctions in Buddhism and the philosophy of religion, for a thesis on Augustine on evil. His recent essays include "Myth, Parable and Truth in Secular Eschatology," "Seeing As, Seeing In and Seeing Through," and "Hindu and Christian Symbols in the Thought of Raimundo Panikkar."

MARK C. TAYLOR is Professor of Religion at Williams College. His books include *Kierkegaard's Pseudonymous Authorship* (1975), *Religion and the Human Image* (co-author, 1977), and *Journeys to Selfhood: Hegel and Kierkegaard* (1980).

CHARLES E. WINQUIST is a Professor of Religious Studies at California State University, Chico. He is the author of *The Transcendental Imagination*, *The Communion of Possibility*, *Homecoming*, and *Practical Hermeneutics*.